This Life

Hour by Hour

A Life and Death Crisis

ALAN OVERLINE

ISBN 978-1-64191-878-7 (paperback)
ISBN 978-1-64191-879-4 (digital)

Copyright © 2018 by Alan Overline

All rights reserved. No part of this publication may be reproduced, distributed, or transmitted in any form or by any means, including photocopying, recording, or other electronic or mechanical methods without the prior written permission of the publisher. For permission requests, solicit the publisher via the address below.

Christian Faith Publishing, Inc.
832 Park Avenue
Meadville, PA 16335
www.christianfaithpublishing.com

Printed in the United States of America

Dedication

I would like to dedicate this book to my dad. For fifty-four years now his life has been a tremendous inspiration to me as to how one should live a Godly life. Actions always speak louder than words and his honesty, forthrightness, and integrity in the way he has and still lives his life are unsurpassed. I can only hope that in my lifetime I will be able to attain the Christ-like values he exhibits continuously day after day.

Words cannot express the gratitude I have to my heavenly Father for giving me the great gift he has given me in my dad. For most of my life, my behavior and trials have tried my dad's patience and love, but, just like my Savior, his love only grew stronger as the years passed. I could only wish that more children on this earth could experience the endless supply of love and understanding that I was shown through such a man of God.

I figure the only way I could ever repay what I feel is such an indebtedness, was to devote my life and my work to both his Father and mine, the Lord Jesus Christ. Had it not been for my dad's unwavering love, you, the reader, would not have this book in your hands.

I would also like to thank a wonderful and devoted Christian, Alvin Kaiser, for his outstanding dedication to the propagation of the Gospel. He was also the financial backer for the writing and completion of this book. The greatest gift by far, though, that I received from Mr. Kaiser over a period of twenty-five years, was the gift of individual evangelism. From the day I met him, he was saving souls. I only wish there were millions like him, sharing Christ at every opportunity in their lives. His consistency is simply Christ-like. There is no other way to describe Alvin's faith. Alvin also deserves much credit for the publication of this message from God to His people.

The Man in the Shell

Once upon a time there was a little boy, who at the tender age of five, built a little shell. The shell was big enough for only him, and the surface was very hard. Something must have scared him, for into the shell he ran:

*He stayed inside and felt secure
Because no one could come in.
The shell was small with little light
So loneliness set in.*

*Afraid of pain outside the shell,
He pondered, should I scout?
But loneliness, his only friend,
Compelled him to come out.*

*The world met him once again
As he went out to play,
To look for friends and be one
Was his only plan that day.*

*He tried so hard to make good friends
But much to his dismay
The very thing which scared him
Sent him on his way!*

*So to the shell, back he went
And entered once again.
Now he knew it was safe to say,
"I lost another friend."*

*The little boy was not aware
Of his created shell,
That every time he entered in
The walls began to swell.*

*Thicker through the years
The walls began to grow
And very soon as you will see
Deep in his life it shows!*

*The little boy was terrified
Very much afraid
Now the boy at age of ten
Began to go astray.*

*The shell became his best old pal.
Degrading words could not come in.
It would be years before he realized
What pain can come from others' sin.*

*In this shell he learned to live
Alone, with all the pain of life,
But where within the shell is room,
For his new-found friend named strife!*

*The inner shell just wouldn't grow
So how could this boy fit?
At twelve years old and growing,
His only choice was sit!*

*So sit he did, in the shell
As fear controlled him on.
Of course, rejection didn't help
Evening, noon 'til dawn.*

One new day outside his shell
In his longing to be free
The path of shame introduced the boy
To his newest friend called whiskey.

What a relief this new friend was
It felt so good to be free.
"I'm out of the shell and I'm not scared.
My friend is right here with me!"

So off he went, his friend and he
To explore outside his shell.
Little did the lost boy know
He was on his way to Hell.

Whiskey lied to him from the beginning
Right from the start,
But a child doesn't know
The devil hates his heart.

After walking with his friend
For just three years or so
Problems suddenly came alive
And streams of tears did flow.

The little frightened child,
Not knowing what to do,
Thought it best by now
If he would just quit school.
So quit he did and ran and hid
Inside his shell once more,
But now at age of seventeen
He began to feel sore.

"I know!" he said to his friend whiskey.
"Let's go take my car.
We can drive forever
After we close the bar!"

So now the wheels began to turn
The wheels of his new life
A life of pain and sorrow,
Loneliness and strife!

When he awoke, he saw the bars
Bars and no way out.
Whiskey and fear had led him
To a thirty-year-long bout.

The walls of institutions
Now became his shell,
But loneliness met with him
In his new small cell.

Prayers went out from his mouth
And all the questions why,
But the only sound which his soul heard
Was the sound of his own cry!

"Alone! Alone!" cried the man.
"What forever have I done?
My friends who lied are now all gone.
Will I ever see the sun?"

"I want to be free!" cried the man
In his agonizing pain.
You've stolen my wife and children,
And my own life you've slain!"

"Where are you, friend who lied to me,
And came and stole my years.
You have left me nothing
But emptiness and tears!"

Loneliness and loss followed him
For many years to come
Until one day the man surrendered
To Christ, God's only son!
Someone said, "He'll set you free
If only you will die!"
So after fighting thirty years,
The lifeless man did cry:

"Oh Lord my God, You sent your Son
To set the prisoners free,
So here I am Lord Jesus Christ
Take every part of me!"

The shell is gone, the fear no more
I laid it by His side
Because now that Christ lives in me
The frightened boy has died!

To tell you all what this means to me
Words can never tell
The only thing I know today
Is that I don't live in a shell!

I'M FREE!!!

Just one more thing I have to say
My old friend Whiskey was by today.
He knocked and knocked till I let him in
And there he stood, Old Black Sin.

"Does the man in the shell live in this house?"
He said.
"I'm sorry, he died. Christ lives here instead!"
If you weren't so blind, you could clearly see
The man lost his shell and found eternity."

Acknowledgements

I want to thank Antonio Jesus Barrientez, who God brought into both my life and my wife's. Our meeting was nothing less than 'Divine Providence'.

Tony is one of God's Angels! After a serious fall injury I sustained in 2007, which left me down and useless for almost five years, and then my wife being diagnosed with a very rare form of Non-Hodgekins Large T-Cell Anaplastic Lymphoma, right when I finally started to recover, our lives fell apart and we lost every material possession we had, including our home of twelve years. At the lowest and most difficult point in our marriage, this man provided for us financially; not only a place to live but replaced both of our lost vehicles with new ones as a gift! But that wasn't enough. He has continued to help support us as my health has still not fully come around. He also funded the publishing and copyright costs of my book and my poetry, "*The Man in the Shell*," my life story at the beginning of this book. His generosity is beyond comprehension! *'The King's heart truly is in the hand of the Lord (Proverbs 21).'*

Without Antonio's love and friendship, you would not be reading this book. Thank you, Tony, for all you've done. We love you with all our hearts. May God richly bless you! This world needs more people like you!

Love Alan & Susan

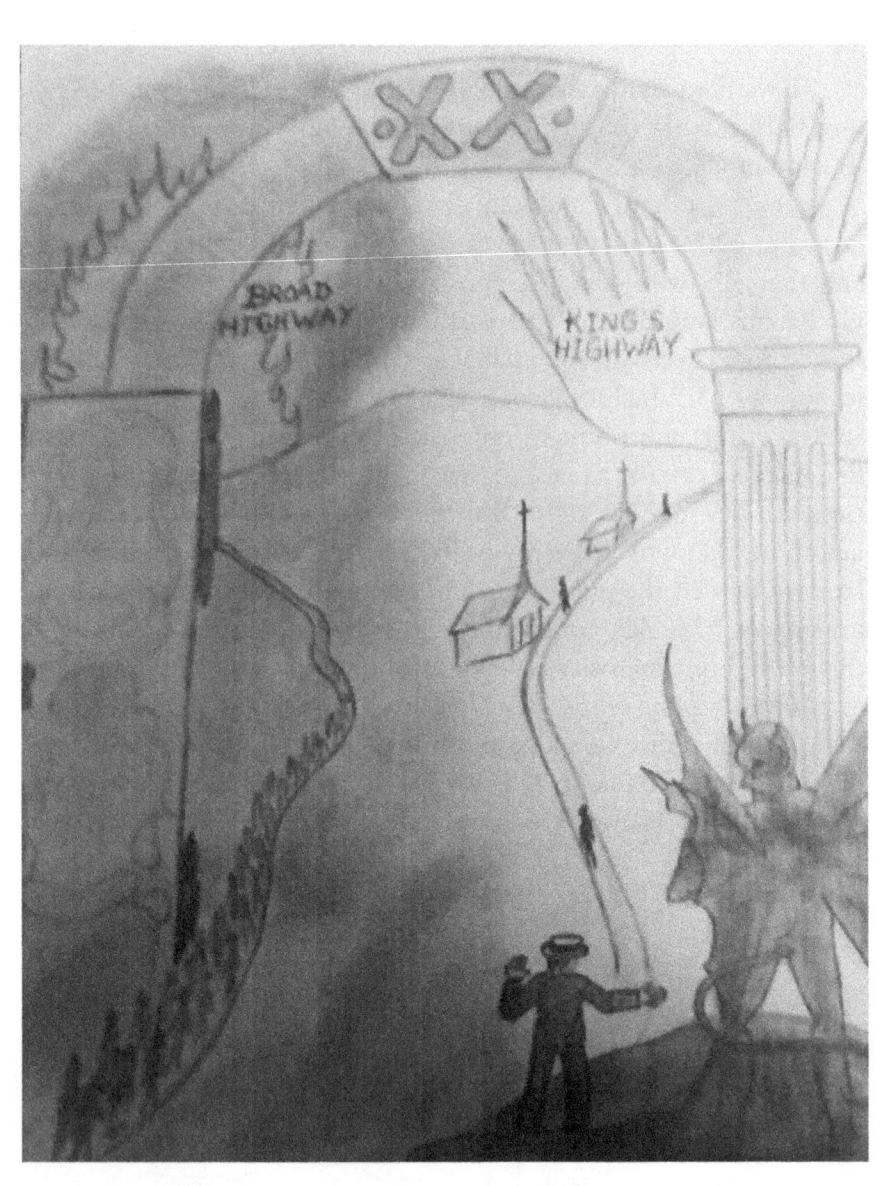

Introduction

My purpose in this book is reformation, especially reformation in the way Christianity is practiced today. American Christians have fed themselves to the full with religion. We have today some of the greatest opportunities to worship and practice our beliefs. In all this grandeur we have forgotten two of the most important issues Christ lived for: lost souls and the power in God's Holy Word.

Due to our selfishness, the Christian population in America since the American Revolution has declined by probably 75%. I'm talking about "fruit-bearing" Christians, those producing names for the Lamb's Book of Life. A lot of people calling themselves Christians are in for a rude awakening when Judgement Day comes.

As a result of America's idolatrous relation to earthly comforts, materialism, and complacency toward religions like Islam, Mormonism, and Jehovah's Witnesses, just to name a few, we are now seeing the beginnings of the "birth pangs" of God's judgement and recompense on a sinful, lazy, and idolatrous nation. Terrorism and groups like Isis are a clear spiritual indicator of what's to come in this generation. God is allowing all this, so take heed, because this may be the last generation of life as we know it!

Within the context of my writing, I have submitted 162 verses of Holy Writ to silence unequivocally any critics. My mentor is Dr. Martin Luther of the sixteenth century, who with the Word of God alone, reformed an entire world of "blind guides leading the blind." It was because of him and his devotion to the truth in God's Word that we, as Christians, can have, hold and read our own personal Bibles today. Thanks, Martin. God bless you!

Sincerely,

Alan K. Overline
12-25-2013

Alan Overline

Notes

Unless specified, Scripture references are from the New American Standard Bible.

1. Psalm 119:99
2. Psalm 119:100
3. Psalm 119:36 (paraphrase mine)
4. Isaiah 54:16
5. Proverbs 16:4
6. Isaiah 14:27
7. Matthew 10:28 (paraphrase mine)
8. Isaiah 10:22
9. Lamentations 1:1
10. Lamentations 1:2
11. Lamentations 1:3
12. Lamentations 1:5
13. Lamentations 1:8
14. Lamentations 1:9
15. Lamentations 1:10
16. Galatians 1:8-9
17. Lamentations 1:14
18. Lamentations 1;15
19. Lamentations 1:16
20. Lamentations 1:17
21. Lamentations 2:2
22. Lamentations 2:5
23. Lamentations 2:13-14
24. Galatians 6:7
25. Lamentations 2:15-17
26. Lamentations 3:20-40
27. Isaiah 6:9-10
28. Philippians 1:6
29. John 9:25

30. Matthew 7:13
31. II Timothy 4:3
32. Romans 1:16
33. James 3:15
34. I Timothy 2:15
35. Romans 10:13-14
36. Matthew 11:12
37. Ephesians 6:12
38. II Corinthians 10:4
39. II Timothy 2:15
40. Matthew 10:39
41. Hebrews 10:31
42. Mark 8:36
43. John 6:63
44. Isaiah 50:7
45. Acts 10:34 (paraphrase mine)
46. Matthew 24:4
47. Matthew 23:38
48. Revelation 3:15-18
49. See *Kingdom of the Cults* by Dr. Walter Martin
50. II Peter 3:9
51. Jeremiah 6:15
52. Romans 1:28
53. Matthew 11:15
54. Philippians 4:13
55. Genesis 6:13
56. II Timothy 2:15 (King James version)
57. Ephesians 6:11
58. Ephesians 6:17
59. II Corinthians 6:2
60. Paraphrase mine
61. Matthew 24:36
62. Hebrews 13:8
63. I Corinthians 2:15
64. II Timothy 2:15
65. II Timothy 2:15 (paraphrase mine)

66. Jeremiah 9:23
67. Philippians 4:7
68. Genesis 15:16
69. Acts 10:34 (paraphrase mine)
70. Numbers 33:52
71. Proverbs 5:21-23
72. Colossians 1:27 (paraphrase mine)
73. Exodus 20:5
74. Job 5:6
75. James 1:21
76. Zachariah 4:6
77. Ecclesiastes 1:14
78. Ecclesiastes 3:11
79. I Corinthians 2:14
80. John 3:30
81. Proverbs 15:33
82. Psalm 119:71
83. Psalm 119:67
84. Philippians 1:6
85. Jeremiah 15:16 (paraphrase mine)
86. Psalm 161
87. II Corinthians 10:3-5
88. Job 23:12
89. Jeremiah 3:20 (paraphrase mine)
90. Psalm 78:49
91. Psalm 83:13-14
92. Psalm 83:1-4
93. Psalm 83:18
94. John 1:1
95. John 14:6
96. Jeremiah 15:16
97. Matthew 13:44
98. Matthew 13:45
99. Philippians 1:21
100. Acts 4:12
101. Hosea 4:6

102. John 14:6
103. I john 4:4
104. John 12:32
105. Luke 11:5
106. Ecclesiastes 9:12
107. Job 1:22
108. Malachi 4:5
109. II Peter 3:9 (paraphrase mine)
110. I Corinthians 2:12-14
111. Ecclesiastes 12:9-14
112. Matthew 9:12-13
113. Luke 15:7
114. Matthew 4:17
115. John 12:32
116. Ecclesiastes 2:26
117. I Corinthians 2:1-5
118. John 6:63
119. John 15:5
120. Hebrews 4:2
121. James 3:1
122. Luke 14:23
123. Matthew 4:4
124. James 2:17 (paraphrase mine)
125. Matthew 25:14
126. Luke 19:11-17
127. Matthew 25:23 (paraphrase mine)
128. Matthew 25:27
129. Matthew 7:21
130. Hebrews 4:12
131. II Timothy 3:17
132. II Peter 1:3
133. II Peter 1:4
134. II Peter 1:3
135. II Peter 1:4
136. II Peter 1:4
137. Ecclesiastes 9:14

138. Colossians 3:16
139. Psalm 90:12
140. Matthew 7:16
141. Proverbs 11:30-31
142. Job 23:12
143. Deuteronomy 6:4-9
144. Deuteronomy 6:7
145. Joshua 24:15 (paraphrase mine)
146. Romans 8:31
147. I John 4:4
148. Isaiah 54:17
149. Psalm 46:2
150. Philippians 1:21
151. I Peter 4:12-14
152. John 14:16
153. Acts 4:12
154. Matthew 15:14
155. II Timothy 4:8
156. Matthew 23:26
157. Matthew 23:27
158. Matthew 23:37-38
159. James 1:27
160. Proverbs 26:11
161. Hebrews 4:12
162. Proverbs 16:16

"This Life; Hour by Hour A Life and Death Crisis"

Hour by hour, the clock keeps ticking, moving forward towards a new day. A day, though, that might not come. What then?

The problem with the clock is that most people wish it would run counterclockwise for a while, but it just keeps on going into the unknown future, and just like everything else, it will stop some day. I'm referring to the clock of this life.

We, as people, intelligent as we have been created to be and as many new innovations as we complete—medical phenomenon, new scientific discoveries, supercomputers, stealth aircraft flying thousands of miles an hour-with all this we still have not been able to stop the clock. We can't slow it down, not even one second.

By the time people truly realize that time cannot be controlled, purchased or reinvented, I'm afraid it will already be too late. Solomon said, *"Moreover, man does not know his time: like a fish caught in a treacherous net and birds trapped in a snare, so the sons of men are ensnared at an evil time when it suddenly falls on them."* (106)

I see a very horrifying future for a world that is so spiritually blind that it laughs at its own horrible fate. We make sport of the future distress without realizing the truth that lies behind many frightening messages that surround us today.

A perfect example of our insidious delusion, which comes instantly to mind, is the television commercial in which a car pulls up to the speaker in the drive-thru at a fast-food restaurant.

The driver says, "Yeah, um, I'd like uh... two, no, make that three weeks and two days and how about a couple of minutes with that too please?"

The next car moves ahead. The driver, typical of today, hurries to a jerky stop and zips down the electric window. He confidently says, "I'll take a couple of days." He hits the accelerator without a confirmation of his order.

The third car pulls up. The driver looks like he works a hundred hours a week, never sees his family, and is totally stressed out. His hair sticks up. He's had a horrifying day at the office and can barely roll down the window. He asks, "Could I have two months?" Then he drives away.

It would be noteworthy to mention at this point the world's mindset, which is running rampant in our midst. Many people laugh at this type of advertisement with a subconscious confidence in relating it to man's extraordinary achievements of creating a quick and easy solution for our problems. In this imaginary instance, man is able to buy lost time at a drive-through window. How convenient that would be. Now if you don't think that people actually have their faith and hope in a future dependent on man's achievements without God, I'm sorry to inform you that you are gravely mistaken. This type of false hope is as prevalent as microwave popcorn.

Many people retain this type of mind-set when they consider only empirical evidence, that which we gain by observation. Unless we also consider revelational evidence, which comes from God, we are likely to view these things in the same manner. A good example of this would be the way Job's wife viewed his calamities and afflictions. She saw and interpreted Job's situation in the flesh. She believed God was being unfair, which would be an acceptable explanation in today's Biblically illiterate society, but it's totally contrary to God's nature which is good and Holy in all He does. Job called her view foolishness.

Job saw the situation with Spiritual eyes and as the Bible says, *"Through all this, Job did not sin, nor did he blame God."* (107)

Quite interesting, isn't it? The eyes of the flesh and the eyes of the Spirit have quite different perceptions, don't they? Imagine the effect of a wrong perception toward eternal life and what the cost might be. Even a blind man will see the judgement seat of Christ.

Now this specific issue of "running out of time" in life, the "end times" or the "end time," nuclear annihilation, or judgement day or the second coming is one that is very broad in the sense that many hundreds, if not thousands, of books have been written on the subject. Some of these writings, occult and otherwise, try to pinpoint the exact date when the end will occur. Still others write and interpret for us end-time prophecies from Ezekiel, Daniel and Revelation, trying to prepare us for *"The great and terrible day of the Lord!"* (108)

How many books will there be? I could try frightening people into a relationship with Christ or intellectually compelling them with lots of neat theology and eschatological doctrines. I could try humor or psychology (which many preachers and writers use today), or spiritual rationalization. But what good would any of this do? Isn't our goal as Christians to reach the unsaved? God's goal is! *"He doesn't wish for anyone to perish in hell. He hopes all will come to repentance for eternal life."* (109) Yet Christians just keep writing all these spiritual books and producing more DVD's series and having more elaborate church functions, including Christian cruises. My, oh my, what a strong religious focus they have for those "Already Saved." Are we not forgetting something, someone?

There are a few vital issues that Christians have seemingly overlooked. These are life-threatening issues from God's Holy Word. Please pay close attention to the focus of the words of St. Paul in his letter to the church at Corinth and how the Holy Spirit spoke to him in regard to the fruitless effort of Christians using super spiritual means in an effort to penetrate a soul which has not first been "born again" in both heart and mind.

It appears from the way the body of Christ today operates that we've put the cart before the horse. What we're doing could be likened to trying to force-feed a mouse a bale of hay. *"Now we* ("We" would be those born-again, Bible-reading Christians of today) *have received not the Spirit of the world, but the Spirit who is from God, that we might know the things freely given to us by God, which things we also speak, not in words taught by human wisdom, but in those taught by the Spirit, combining Spiritual thoughts with Spiritual words* (an understanding of the next words are vital in dealing with lost souls). *But a "natural man" does not accept the things of the Spirit of God;* (of which things we write and sing and preach about) *for they are 'foolishness' to him and he cannot understand them, because they are Spiritually appraised."* (110)

Therefore, in close review of these "Holy Ghost-inspired" words of the Saint, I ask you, what good do all the Spiritual books in the world and all the joyous songs and Christian music and all the greatest sermons and cassette tapes do for the "man of a "natural mind" since they are "foolishness" to him and he "cannot" understand them. What we have, then, is a lot of wasted effort and wasted vital time, all because of self-serving thinking–all directed to those already saved.

Is the picture growing clearer yet? Let me continue.

Please listen carefully to the words of the wisest man who ever lived, King Solomon, and take heed from what HE says about using words of persuasion, eloquence of speech and reading and writing multiple books: *"In addition to being a wise man, the preacher* (himself) *also taught the people knowledge; and he pondered, searched out and arranged many proverbs. The preacher sought to find delightful words* (as do we authors and preachers) *and to write the words of truth correctly. The words of wise men are like goads* (something that urges or prods to provoke movement) *and the masters of these collections are like well-driven nails, they are given by one shepherd. But beyond this, my son,* (us) *be warned: the writing of many books is endless and excessive devotion to books is wearying to the body. The conclusion, when all has been heard is, fear God and keep His commandments, because this applies to every person. For God will bring every act to judgement, everything which is hidden, whether it is good or evil."* (111)

Now, these words are pretty profound and straightforward, are they not? So now I ask the Christian reader again, what good do all the greatest pulpit sermons and all the dynamic teaching series and all the Christian self-help books and expositions in the whole world do for the "man of the natural mind," the UNSAVED, surrounding us on every continent of the globe? Was not the main focus of our efforts, demonstrated by our Lord Himself in His ministry, directed to the lost sheep? *"It is not those who are healthy who need a physician, but those who are sick* (Spiritually sick). *But go and learn what this means, I desire compassion, and not sacrifice, for I did not come to call the righteous but sinners."* (112)

The Lord's mission was not those who were saved but specifically the LOST. The Christian mission today seems to focus the majority of its efforts on building up the "already righteous." If we just took a third of our efforts and focused them only on the unsaved, the results would be astounding.

The last Christian group in Minnesota here that I recall making a specific attempt at person-to-person evangelism out on the streets and wherever Divine Providence led did so twenty-five years ago. I haven't seen one since. Even that attempt was a sad state of affairs, as any one of the individuals I recall involved would simply have been devoured by any twenty-one-year-old Mormon or Jehovah's Witness. Why? Because they were biblically illiterate. The intentions were pure, but the results were vague. I will address "good intentions" later.

Again, now let me bolster my theme as I quote directly from the mouth of Jesus Himself. *"I tell you that in the same way, there will be more joy in heaven over one sinner who repents, than over ninety-nine righteous persons who need no repentance."* (113)

Repentance was, without any question, the number one issue always at the forefront of Christ's ministry. What is ours? The very first words coming out of Christ's mouth at the very start of His mission on earth were *"REPENT, for the Kingdom of heaven is at hand!"* (114)

John the Baptist was the same way. The Pharisees came for baptism and the first words out his mouth (Matthew 3:8) demanded repentance.

You see, then, that all the Spiritual books and the like in the universe, other than God's Holy life-giving Word are useless to the "natural minded" man. These multiple books and sermons, teaching series and seminars are wonderful for the strengthening of a saved man's faith. Such a man can already understand and retain "by faith" what he hears and reads. I use these books often myself, but, without question, the one I use most is God's Holy Word. After all, it was His Word on the printed page, which drew me to the cross and repentance. It is the power of Life in the Word, alone which is my entire focus in writing to you today. My point is simple, just like Christ, always simple, and yet so very profound. There is nothing, absolutely nothing, in this world, contained within itself that has enough power to give life and open the Spiritual eyes, ears and minds than God's wonderful, majestic, awesome and glorious Word.

My purpose again and foremost God's purpose in this message will be to show how God's Word itself can, will, and has changed every conceivable life issue and circumstance imagined. Then I will compel any unsaved readers of this message to devote themselves fully to the Holy Word of God so they too can share in and understand with a new mind the rich and wonderful promises and blessings God has in store for them.

I'm not going to try to lead anyone from Genesis to Revelation with my own paraphrase of the Scriptures. Too many books have already been written and messages given about the Holy Bible with the purpose of sticking the Bible's meaning, bit by bit, piece by piece, into the minds of "natural men." You see, other preachers, teachers, and authors know as well as I do that the vast majority of people do not read the Bible themselves. In vain many leaders of our faith continually try to spoon feed people the Word. Instead of giving it to the "natural minded" in this way, let's bring them to the entire book, not pieces of the book to them throughout their lifetime. If we give the entire Word, God's power will do the rest.

Yes, we want to nurture and teach new Christians, by all means, but one must be first rooted and grounded in God's Word, not ours. As I stated before and will do again, the Words of our Lord speak for themselves. *"If I be lifted up from the earth, I will draw all men unto me!"* (115) Remember, Jesus is the Word. If we lift up his Word, He will cause the growth.

Now let's return to good intentions.

Most people have good intentions, but too often they use them in the wrong direction and toward the wrong people. At least that's the impression I get when I study the two verses I quoted earlier from I Corinthians 2:12-14. It's more than an impression. That's why I feel the urgency of this message. The Holy Spirit wouldn't even let me sleep. I grew sick and tired of preaching to myself.

The whole theory of multiple and more knowledgeable books and more in-depth sermons is like sand running through our fingers– if our focus is the unsaved as our Lord's was. King Solomon would have said, *"For this too is vanity and striving after the wind!"* (116)

The words of St. Paul ring deep in my Spirit as I see him constantly directing our focus away from men and their wisdom to the wisdom and power of God. His focus was also not in glorifying himself as a great and fluent preacher but seeing to it that that the One who could bring sinners eternal life was exalted and glorified. Take heed, my dearest readers, to I Corinthians chapter 2:1-5.

"And when I came to you brethren, I did not come with the superiority of speech or of wisdom, proclaiming to you the testimony of God. For I determined to know nothing among you except Jesus Christ, and Him crucified. And I was with you in fear and in much trembling. And my message and my preaching were not in persuasive words of wisdom, but in demonstration of the Spirit and of power, that your faith SHOULD NOT rest on the wisdom of men, but on the power of God." (117)

I guess if one's faith is not to rest on the wisdom of men, then that only leaves one other entity on which to solidify our faith: God, Christ, His Word. Since His Word is readily available, I guess that gives us all a pretty simple conclusion as to our source of Life which we, as Christians, are to impart to others. The Word is King, literally.

I could easily quote a hundred quick scripture verses to support my position as to what's missing in our Christian mission on earth, but again, my purpose and God's for this message is not to get bits and pieces of the Bible down on these pages so maybe a non-Christian will get a quick eye-full of the Word and then seemingly have a good change of heart, which will last only as long as his "natural mind" will retain it. Makes good sense, doesn't it?

My purpose is to persuade non-Christians toward one, and only one, book, the Bible, so they can read it for themselves. Then and only then will there be consistency in Christian growth for all who truly seek Him. And what can thwart the Word of God? Well, Satan tries desperately, but the 'rightly divided' Word of Truth spoken in power and faith leaves our foe powerless and defeated. The Word of God cuts Satan like a knife. That's precisely why Jesus quoted it to him three times in His desert temptation and Satan left, head down, tail between his legs.

The reason the Word of God implanted in one's soul will bring consistency in Christian growth is the same reason Jesus was consistent and without sin. The Word of God, the Bible itself, and nothing else offered to us by man, is the only book on earth which can give life and even raise people from the dead. Jesus and the Word are synonymous.

John 6:63 says, *"It is the Spirit who gives life, the flesh profits nothing. The Words that I have spoken to you are Spirit and life."* (118) Jesus himself tells us here in this straightforward passage of Scripture who and what gives life, eternal life. It is the Spirit. But wait. How does Jesus define this "Spirit" which gives life? And what does He say about the flesh? It PROFITS NOTHING. It produces no souls for the Kingdom of God; no names for the Lambs Book of Life.

What does Jesus tell us in John 15:5? "I am the vine. You are the branches; he who abides in Me, and I in him, together we bring forth much fruit; for apart from Me you can do nothing." (119) Jesus clearly indicates here that the only people bringing forth fruit (saved souls) are those living (abiding) in his Word, the Scriptures. Abiding in Jesus and the Word are one and the same. See John 1:1.

Therefore, people, if, as in John 6:63, it is the Spirit who gives life to lost souls and the Spirit is defined as "the Words which I (Jesus) have spoken," then let us give all people in our lives and acquaintances His Word, the Bible, and give them life. Also, keep in mind, "No man can live on bread alone, but only on every Word that proceeds from the mouth of God." In other words, we need the whole, entire, complete Word of God.

The opposite of life is death, in a church as well as in a person. I'm sad to say that I see a lot of dead people in and outside the body of Christ today. If you're not spiritually alive, you're dead. The same is true for a church. Without Christ in you, the eternal Hope of glory, you're already dead.

The body of Christ is suffering severely, all from a lack of personal devotion to God's Word. This goes for preachers and lay people alike. I think people would have a better chance for the abundant life in Christ and making their way to heaven if they were to soak their shorts in gasoline and run through the fire pits of hell than to find eternity through man's books, cassettes, tape series, and church visits one or two hours a week listening to fallible man.

Do you realize how many people get out of church and into their cars and immediately begin to argue and fight about some stupid issue of the flesh, as if they had just walked out of a saloon or nightclub on a Saturday night. Don't kid yourself. It happens all the time. Not much fruit has come to bear on the branch whose vine is his own "natural mind."

Without personal digestion, dedication and devotion to the Bible itself, there is absolutely no transformation from flesh to the New Birth of the Spirit. There is no hope whatsoever to stand against our enemy. You might just as well put on your gasoline-soaked shorts and run for it.

A true faith in God must precede our ability to benefit from the preaching of God's Word through any man or book or teaching. And where does faith come from? The Word of God. Please, my dear readers, receive the following words as food for your souls and understand the problems we face in bringing people to Christ. We can't just go out and do things our own way anymore. We must consider and consult God's wisdom in order to be successful in evangelizing. "For we have had Good News preached to us, just as they (the "natural minded") also; but the Word which they heard DID NOT profit them because it not united by Faith in those who heard!" (121) I can't say it any plainer than Hebrews 4:2 just said it.

There is a good Spiritually logical reason why in 228 years America's gone from independence and safety to becoming a slave to sin and left unprotected from destruction. It's time for Christian America, what is left of it anyway, to wake up and cherish God's Word again.

Did not our Lord and Savior Jesus Christ say through the words of His brother James, *"Let not many of you become teachers, my brethren, knowing that as such we shall incur a stricter judgement!?"* (121) This is a huge responsibility given to those teaching God's Word. Are we not all teachers who bear the name of Christ? Whether through our words or actions, certainly a message is taught. We, as Christians, have a great responsibility to these unsaved people and we will be held responsible if we don't do our jobs. We must remember, this job cannot be done in our own wisdom or strength. It is only possible through God's Word and the power of the Holy Spirit. Power is perfected in weakness and surrender. Only an empty vessel void of fleshly desires and filled with the Holy Spirit is an effective vessel in doing God's work.

We need to make it our priority and start informing people of the vitalness of personal and individual devotion and dedication to God's Word, America's and the world's only hope. The book of James warns us good intentions don't save lives. The road to hell was paved with good intentions. We need to become alert and compel them toward resurrection. It's that vital. It's absolutely imperative. We must compel them!

Jesus commanded us to do it in His parable concerning unsaved souls in Luke 14. The Lord showed anger in verse 21 when the report came back to Him that all the invitations for the dinner were given out, but yet there were still empty seats, in heaven that is. There were souls who had missed out on salvation.

And what was our Lord's response to this terrible sight of unsaved people rejecting the offer of salvation? Verse 23 says it explicitly. "Go out into the highways and along the hedges and compel them to come in that My house may be filled!" (122)

I don't see many Christians in America along the hedges these days. Although there's plenty of Mormon's leading people down the wide road of destruction. There are millions in the churches but the hedges have been left for the devil to groom into any nature he desires. Turn on your TV set and tell me I'm wrong. Count all the kids, eighteen and under, doing life sentences in adult prisons. Some will kill for a pair of sneakers! Most people just don't care anymore!

I would like to briefly share with the reader a statement made by a close friend of my family, who was born in the late 1890's and lived ninety-nine years.

He lived through the great depression and traveled all over the United States as a circus performer and owner of a circus. He was a great artist, inventor, and professional animal trainer who traveled with hobos on trains and went hungry so many times you couldn't count it. Simply, he was an amazing human being! He also loved children. He was a God-fearing man who worked for the rich at times and lived with the poor most of his life.

Before he died in 1989, when asked about his morals and religious beliefs, he stated, "When I was a boy, Belle Plaine, Minnesota had carbon-fueled hanging street lamps. I was amazed to see how the moths would fly into the flame. By morning, there would be thousands of dead moths on the ground under the light. I thought, how stupid! Today permissiveness is like a flame and people act just as stupid as moths. They run into this flame and many are destroyed. Permissive with no morals, thinking they will find happiness. No wonder young people, when they see older people's actions don't follow them." I guess I don't need to add to that except to tell the reader this man only had a sixth-grade education! He had 'spiritual eyes' though! He loved God. His focus was the lost!

By the way, has anyone seen the new hit, "Queer Eye for the Straight Guy"? These types of shows today are actually referred to in the TV industry as "must see TV." I personally have never been so offended in all my life when I see what our society has allowed the media to display on TV to our children, God's children. I used to have a vast worldly vocabulary to describe human beings whom, mindlessly and with hearts of granite, exploit, condone and promote iniquity and abominable behavior, but now that Christ lives in me, I won't be using them to describe these sorts. Does anyone truly care anymore about what's being done to the hearts and minds of our children?

Now back to Luke 21; The word "compel" was chosen by our Lord in the Gospel of Luke for a good reason, just like every other word in the Holy Writ. I must again, by necessity, repeat the Words of Christ; *"Man cannot live on bread alone* (worldly sustenance), *but on every word that proceeds from the mouth of God."* (123) We, as Christians, need not only digest every word of the Holy Bible but we must act on it. Remember, *"Faith without works is dead!"* (124) Faith without work's, people, does not contain one ounce of eternal significance. I probably should have titled this book **Eternal Significance** because, truly, that should be the constant theme of our thinking, preaching, and living as God's people.

"Compel" is a strong word. It carries a great sense of urgency. Almost forceful, it means "to press." Whenever I read that command in God's Word, I can just see the look on Jesus' face. I can see the enormous concern for just one lost soul, one of His lost sheep straying in the wilderness of a wicked, deceptive world waiting to be destroyed by the evil one. His heart saddens and tears fill His eyes, as he cries out loudly to Himself, "My book of life must be filled! Please, please, my people, compel these, My lost children to come home so that we all may rejoice!"

This world is vast and complex. Only a Sovereign and Mighty God could have created something so awesome and wondrous. Now think for a moment, if you will, about the fact that God gave us dominion over the entire universe. He has trusted us to take care of His world, including and most importantly, the souls that dwell here. Are we going to let Him down like the unfaithful servant who buried the talent in the ground did? This servant gave back to His master only that which he was given in the first place.

It's obvious in the Scriptures that Christ expects more. He expects more souls, more fruits of our talents. These talents, which he has given us, have eternal implications. The Lord (represented by the slave owner in Matthew 25:14) was so angry that he said to the negligent, self-preserving servant, *"You wicked, lazy slave, you knew that I reap where I did not sow."* (125) The fact that Christ used the words, "you knew," leaves all lazy, self-serving people without excuse. In the parable in Luke 19:11-27, the Lord uses much stronger language when he says, *"But these enemies of Mine, who did not want Me to reign over them, bring them here and slay them in my presence."* (126) Don't delude yourselves Christians. This is the New Testament I'm talking about! Not the law! How long would even an earthly boss leave you with your job if you ignored his commands? Hello?

Now I've been going to church for half a century, including my prison time) and I don't ever recall hearing a sermon or teaching, other than my own, on the parable of the talents. This type of direct and honest preaching, including issues concerning the judgement and righteous indignation of our Lord on issues, is almost non-existent in our churches in America today. You hear the other half of the Gospel most anywhere, but what's happened to the other half?

Jesus almost always had a two-fold message, the promise of blessing and the warning of judgement. Our one-sided preaching and its effect on all America is shown clearly in our willingness as a nation to compromise with the filth surrounding us today. Yes, Christians have a voice in America today, but do you hear it? Is anyone hearing it? Are your children and grandchildren hearing the voice of God through you?

We all need to decide if we are individually going to fully use, to the best of our abilities, the gifts that God has given each of us for bringing people to Christ and saving souls. Will we help others to look toward His glorious and triumphant return when He will say as he did to the man who turned the five talents into ten, *"Well done, my good and faithful servant, enter now into the Kingdom of Joy."* (128) Jesus said, *"For to everyone who has shall more be given and he shall have an abundance,* (spiritual truth and a desire to use it) *but from the one who does not have fruits, even what he does have shall be taken away!"* (128)

Another reminder of Spiritual reality is given by our Lord when He says plainly, "Not everyone who says to Me. 'Lord, Lord,' will enter the Kingdom of heaven, but he who does the will of My Father, who is in heaven." (129) In other words, not all who address themselves as Christians and talk the Christian talk are going to heaven.

Two hundred plus years of compromise within Christendom in America have left a lot of blind people in for a big surprise when Christ returns. Those who simply cater to themselves can hardly be considered Christian. We might as well stop trying to fool each other. God sees everything and I mean everything! He hears everything too. If you want peace, you won't find it with what the world has to offer so quit looking there. Ask a Haitian Christian where the joy comes from – it's not anything of this world!

Because of our lack of discipline to God's Word and devoted study of it in its entirety, we as Christians and our purpose here on earth are being utterly defeated. If we don't believe this, all we have to do is go to our local church and ask for a show of hands of how many unsaved newcomers sit among us at our Sunday service. The hands in the air would show us the truth. This is embarrassing. Many aspire but few attain!

Or perhaps I could pose the question of how many people this past week, month or even year, shared Christ with someone they didn't know or perhaps someone they did know but who was unsaved? I'm not here to embarrass anyone. I'm here for God to let you know what is on His mind and the message is... "Get moving!" When you present yourself before the throne on judgement day, would you offer your Lord a rotten apple for fruit? When I stand before God, I shall say, "Lord, behind me, these souls Father - men, women and children, these are the gifts I bring Thee!"

Today is the day of salvation says the Lord. We should not wait for a day when we finally muster up enough courage. God gives shameless courage every day if we know deeply His Word in our hearts. It's much easier to witness in God's power, folks, but there's only one place to get that power. That place is in the Holy Word of God. When individuals begin to cherish and treasure God's Word, when they finally realize that it's *"living and active,"* (130) and all-powerful in changing sinners into saints, when they realize that there is no greater gift on the face of the earth that one can give another than God's Word, then they become mature in Christ.

People need to stop treating Christianity as some sort of upper echelon-private club for members only. It seems to me that the Holy Ghost's hunger for souls, which permeated Christ's being, has been lost to busy time schedules and personal pampering. The effect of America's time-consuming pampering and self-indulgence has made the difference between the casual reading of the Holy Scriptures and devoted study of it. The results of the negligence surround God's people, both in their homes and personal lives. The Word of God is not a devotional. It is our daily bread to sustain us to do Gods work.

America's lack of holiness has diminished God's Holiness. Be sure, though, that the reader understands that God's Holiness is only diminished in the minds of self-preserving people who neglect God's commands. The lazy, forgetful, wayward people of God are sure to be speechless in the presence of God's grand Holiness. Boy, oh boy, are the Muslims in for a surprise if they don't acknowledge Christ as King and their only Savior. For these Muslims, Judgement Day without Christ will truly be a Holy and righteous Jihad (holy war).

We Christians need to "beef up" more on Holy Scripture and less on all this media exercise and health craze. What benefits a lost soul more? Your physical state or your Spiritual state? Your relationship to the health club or to God?

We must never forget Christian brothers and sisters, that Jesus became like us so that we could become like Him in word and deed. He was our example to follow.

There is a difference between the casual reading of the Scripture only to silence our own consciences and devoted study of it in its entirety so as to be *"adequate and equipped for every good work,"* (131) as Paul reminded Timothy. II Peter 1:3-4 tells us that God has made available to anyone who desires, *"Everything pertaining to Life and Godliness, through the true knowledge of Him."* (132) Not something, EVERYTHING!

The place I'm urgently trying to get everyone who reads these pages is to spend more time in THE WORD OF GOD. Peter goes on to say that it is through God's *"precious and magnificent promises* (the Word again) *that one escapes the corruption that is in the world by lust!"* (133) The word *lust* in Greek denotes "to set the heart upon, to long for, or intense craving." I think that definition does great justice in describing America's desires for that which does not profit the Kingdom of God. If we truly want to separate our hearts and minds in order to dedicate them to God, then Peter tells us the way to escape our flesh, which is constantly warring against our Spirit, and that again is the Word of God, or as Peter refers to it, God's *"Precious and magnificent promises* (134). Everything goes right back to the Book. All of God's power is in the Book. The Word of God is the Father's glory and excellence."

If someone were to ask me, "How does one describe God's glory so as to truly understand it?" I would answer, "That's simple. God's glory is nothing less than His Son Jesus Christ and his devotion to the eternal purposes of His Father and that purpose is the salvation of the souls of all mankind. This is God's glory! "In nothing is the Father, our Father, more glorified! When we, as Christians, strive and sacrifice our lives, time and money in order to fill the Lamb's Book of Life with the names of those who are lost and without eternal life, then we also become God's glory. We then become, as Peter says, *"Partakers of the Divine Nature!"* (135)

There is also a great truth to be learned from the opposite of the above truth. When we lust or set our hearts upon or long for that which doesn't promote Spiritual growth, we then become partakers in the world's corruption. In order to escape this curse, we must long for and set our hearts upon *"His precious and magnificent promises!"* (136)

The knowledge of God is intimacy with His purposes. From knowledge comes power, Divine power! For here again, all of God's power is available to us in the Word of God. All of this may begin to sound redundant, dear reader, but for this, I make no apologies. This pen won't stop until God beseeches me to stop. It seems there is a bit more yet that needs to be said.

I have always been a person with a very fervent spirit. I have never been known to compromise. Whether it be for good or for bad, I have always given a one hundred percent effort. I've never been lukewarm. It's either hot or cold. The very fact that God has knocked on my heart's door to deliver this "not so gentle" message tells me only one thing; He means business. God did not give us life to own every new electronic device that seems to come out once a month or to make sure your house is one thousand square feet bigger than your neighbors. He gave us life to ensure others have it too, eternally. Material things are fine as long as they don't hinder Gods work. Mostly, they do!

One of my favorite Bible verses has always been *"Whatever your hand finds to do, verily, do it with all your might; for there is no activity or planning or wisdom in Sheol (the grave) where you are going.* (137) Believe me, this message is just like fire shut up in my bones. The zeal of the Lord has consumed me and I'm coming after you for the glory of God. Let His name be exalted on all the earth!

I often wished people thought of the Bible as they do their American Express cards. They don't leave home without it. Membership has its privileges. Many people don't even bring their Bibles to church. I know of a lot of Bibles being used for centerpieces or for dust collectors. I think that going to church without your Bible is like going to a restaurant without your mouth.

Consider for a moment if you will, what would happen if at this very moment all the Bibles in the world vanished or were destroyed or banned by an enemy? How long would it be before Christianity was wiped off the face of the earth? A few years maybe? How would you train your children in righteousness without God's Word? How would you defend your heart and mind from the attacks of Satan, who knows and misquotes Scripture to suit his purposes to build cults worldwide, endangering our faith? How would pastors prepare a new message each Sunday? I have a good foolproof suggestion: write the Bible on your heart. Conceive it there. Pray that the Holy Spirit may give birth to it in your heart. Colossians 3:16 says, *"Let the Word of Christ richly dwell within you."* (138) One must let it live there and grow to fruition. Be mature in Christ. Receive the power from on High, the excellent and glorious life of Christ, our Savior and risen Lord. Become a part of the Father's glory, here and now today, for tomorrow you may never see.

Even in the oldest Psalm of the Psalter written by Moses, we see divine wisdom in his words. *"So teach us to number our days, that we present to thee a heart of wisdom."* (139) Moses well knew that we must one day present ourselves to God and give an account of how we used our time and for whom. He considered the brevity of life. In America, people live as though they will live on Earth forever. But in that assumption, they are dead wrong! Moses desires here in Psalm 90:12 to present to God a heart of wisdom at the end of life. What is a "heart of wisdom" other than having a heart's desire to fill the Lamb's Book of Life as Christ did as the epitome of God's glory?

An eternal focus with each day we live presents to God a heart of wisdom. The book you're reading is the sole result of a heart of wisdom gained only by the grace of God, through faith in His Word. People who love the Word of God can easily be recognized by their eternal focus and desire to win souls.

Jesus himself says, *"You shall know them by their fruits."* (140) King Solomon goes one step further in confirming my words when he says, *"The fruit of the righteous is a tree of life, and he who is wise wins souls. If the righteous* (soul winners) *will be rewarded in the earth, how much more true that the wicked and the sinner shall get what they deserve!"* (141)

Without the Word of God implanted, which is able to save our souls, neither can we save other souls and win them to Christ. Without God's Word re-exalted in America as the most important of all our concerns, we are finished as a Christian nation. Our cause and Christ's desire that none would perish might as well have slipped into the sea.

A lack of respect and reverence for God's word is still permeating Christian circles today. I'll never forget how devastated I was at a Christian Christmas party for bible college students even as far back as 1986. I was a student and upon entering a private home a few of the other students approached me. They whispered, "Now, Al, let's not talk about the Bible tonight. We hear enough of that at school."

If that's how students at a Bible college feel, they are wasting space there. Obviously, they didn't know what I enjoyed more than life itself.

"Al, promise me you won't start in, O.K."

My first reaction was on the inside of my heart and spirit. It felt as if I was being crushed by a satanic worldly spirit. I almost wanted to cry for my Lord. I just solemnly nodded and walked in. More than one thing crossed my mind. Believe me, I was in deep Spiritual pain and somewhat angry. What is Christmas? Is there not a Divine message and purpose for this majestic occasion? What is fellowship if not to edify one another in the Word of God that we may be of good service to our Savior? Then again in retrospect, if people are offended at the Word taking up too much of their time, they probably wouldn't have had much to offer in the way of new testimonies anyway.

I always have had something to share about Christ. I still do today, 365 - 24 - 7. Just try me! The Word of God in me is like a mighty river, which never stops flowing and never sees drought. I can't help talking about Christ. It makes absolutely no difference where I am or who is listening. Actually, I love it when strangers are listening. It could very well be the seed that Christ waters and saves that person's soul. You just don't know.

After my incident with the Russian cab driver, Oleg, I knew that I wasn't concerned about anything but planting the seeds from there on out. God is truly faithful. If you're not seeing fruits of new names written down in glory, then there's simply something wrong with your relationship to God's Word. I would suggest that much of the cause of this fruitlessness is the lack of Christ's true vision and purpose because our minds are so full of worldly concerns that we have no room left to retain or store Truth.

Our hearts have been taken captive by self. There may not be any "full-serve" gas stations left in America, but there is plenty of "self-serve" to make up for it. America is the king of "self-serve." The only problem is that salvation is not for sale. People try to sell salvation just as people try to sell anything and everything today. Christ and His gift are free, free for the asking. When will people learn?

When that particular individual at the Christmas party asked me point blank not to talk about the Bible, I was just tormented. I don't think I've ever heard such a worldly statement from a Christian in all my life. Are these not the words of the heathen? What are these colleges teaching these days? Christianity, folks, is not a "mind" thing. It's a heart thing. If the Word of God only goes as far as one's mind, it's of no value to the eternal purposes of God's plan and Kingdom. Job said, *"I have not departed from the command of His lips; I have treasured the Words of His mouth more than my necessary food!"* (142) I guess Job's words should be a grand indicator of the importance of God's Word in our lives.

Is it any wonder why we have such a defeated people in the body of Christ today? It's simply that people see the Word of God as just another commodity or something. They only use it in the right setting or place. To do this is totally contrary to God's Word. How would Jesus have answered the gentleman at the Christmas party? Listen to Deuteronomy 6:4-9, "The Shema" (pronounced smååh) of the Jewish people. No one, Gentile or Jew, is exempt from this great section of Scripture, or any other part of Scripture, for that matter.

"Hear, O Israel! The Lord is our God and the Lord is One! And you shall love the Lord your God with all your heart and all your soul and all your might. And these words which I am commanding you today

shall be on your heart; and you shall teach them diligently to your sons and shall talk of them when you sit in your house and when you walk by the way and when you lie down and when you rise up. And you shall bind them as a sign on your hand and they shall be as frontals on your forehead. And you shall write them on the doorposts of your house and on your gates." (143)

I don't know about the reader, but the impression I get from those verses is that the Word of God should always be the focus of our conversation everywhere at all times. There is a lot to be learned from this set of verses. Did not Jesus take verse 5 and call it the first and greatest commandment? Yes, he did. He just added the phrase, "with all your might." We can find this quote in Mark 12:30.

You can see here how the Lord gave us instruction on how to successfully and I repeat "successfully" love the Lord with all your heart, soul and might. We can love the Lord very simply. All we have to do is continually and constantly discuss God's Word. We can build up and edify one another, even strangers.

As the Word says, "Even when you walk by the way!" (144) Street evangelism is great when led by the Holy Spirit. Do you find yourself, Mr. and Mrs. Christian, in general meetings among new acquaintances, as you **walk by the way**, talking about your Savior? In the supermarket, at the laundromat, in the bowling alley or even at an exclusive country club after eighteen holes? Or do you save it for Sunday mornings, home Bible studies or maybe the yearly retreat?

The point is folks that we need to set a standard. This standard has been missing for centuries. We need to restore theocracy, which is a Biblically centered universe. We can begin this restoration through lives like yours and mine. Until we, as members of the Body of Christ, start doing our share, crime rates and terrorism will rise until we have no escape.

If the falling of the Twin Towers didn't wake people up, I'm afraid the hardening of men's hearts may be beyond redemption.

America's heart reminds me so much of Pharaoh. He just didn't want change regardless of the consequences. God did harden His heart. However, has this now happened to us? Maybe the best thing New York could have done is leave the burnt remains of the buildings in place. It certainly is typical of America, though, to clean the mess up as fast as we did. Out of sight, out of mind. Except for the victim's families. They won't soon forget.

"Choose you this day whom you will serve, America."

"As for me and my house, we will diligently serve the Lord" (145) each day of our lives. My time is for God's use. I wasted enough of my life on things of the flesh. The Word saved my life. It has also brought life to many I've shared with. This was eternal life, not temporary happiness.

God gives all his children opportunities to share with others His glory. God isn't just looking for ability. He wants availability. God has all the ability in the universe to impart if he deems it necessary to do so. All he needs is empty vessels, vessels of honor and integrity, humility and holiness, contrite and willing, dedicated and devoted, to answer His every call day or night.

Approximately ten years ago, when God revealed his message to me, I recall reading somewhere what I deemed at that time a great truth for that day, yet today it "fits the bill" for America far better than in 1994. The statement read as follows: "It's no more a mystery why such churches have lost their Holy influence and their warmth of Spiritual life, while worldliness flourishes from the pew to the pulpit"

People today don't want to talk about religion in public, especially not about Jesus. Someone might laugh or persecute them. They don't say that "Name" in public. This has been my experience. I see it with so-called Christians all the time. I always thought that *"If God is for us, who is against us?"* (146) *"Greater is he who is in you than he who is in the world."* (147) *"No weapon that is formed against you shall prosper."* (148) *"Therefore, we will not fear, though the earth should change, and though the mountains slip into the heart of the sea."* (149) With promises like these is there any need or even room for fear and rejection?

I tell every one of you reading or hearing this message, if you're not willing to take up your cross, along with the pain and scars of suffering for the name of Jesus Christ, that His name may be exalted in all the earth, along with the insults and persecution on account of your beliefs, then don't call yourself a Christian. This would be a shame to the glorious name of Christ. It's an abomination unto the Lord. *"To live is Christ, to die is gain!"* (150) He who loves his life shall lose it, saith the Lord.

"Beloved, do not be surprised at the fiery ordeal among you, which comes upon you for your testing, as though some strange things were happening to you; but to the degree that you share the sufferings of Christ, keep on rejoicing, so that also at the revelation of His glory, you may rejoice with exultation. If you are reviled for the name of Christ, you are blessed, because the Spirit of Glory and of God rests upon you." (151)

In the Roman Catholic Church of centuries past, the theory was forced upon people that only the priest holding a doctorate degree in Divinity could properly interpret Scripture. Many theories still held today are nothing but imaginations of religious spirits and power-seeking men and institutions grasping for positions of authority in the Kingdom of God. They have no Scriptural or Apostolic basis. A perfect example of this would be a long-held tradition within Catholicism that the Pope or the Papacy is the present "vicar" of Christ. They believe, as direct descendants of the Apostle Peter, (which again is nonsense) that they hold the power of the keys or control the office of the Kingdom of God on earth until Christ returns. This is also nonsense! Even in regard to Scripture interpretation within Catholicism today, there seems to be an improper veneration of the priest's ability and wisdom in regard to the handling, reading, understanding, and teaching of Holy Scripture.

All this, in the veneration of ignorance, has caused Spiritual blindness among millions of Biblically illiterate people who now strive to work their way into heaven. Such a plan is an impossibility. We are simply saved by grace through faith in Christ. Good works are a by-product of Christ in us, not of us!

The veneration of the Mother Mary and the Saints has long been an idolatrous invention of man, fully condemned in Scripture and certainly no way to communicate to our heavenly Father. Such nonsense has gone on long enough! How long will we leave our brothers and sisters in the dark? How can we, unless totally blind, twist the Scripture in John 14:16, which says, *"I* (Jesus himself is speaking) *am the way and the truth and the life; NO ONE comes to the Father but through Me!"* (152)

I don't know how a person can ignore such a great and straightforward truth. Does this not unequivocally exclude Mary and the Pope, who are nothing more than mere man, woman, or any of the saints or any other man, for that matter? "No one" means NO ONE! Neither the Pope nor Mary was ever crucified nor had their bloodshed as a sacrifice for all humanity. Does the Scripture lie? God knows the heart of those praying to Mother Mary and knows their sincerity, but the problem still exists that it's learned tradition over centuries and is simply Idol worship in plain terms. It has no scriptural basis. Praying the rosary over and over again is vain repetition and the scripture says NOT to pray this way as the Gentiles do!

Does not Luke tell us clearly in Acts 4:12 that *"There is salvation in no one else; for there is no other name under heaven that has been given among men, by which we must be saved!"* (153) Need I say more? The scripture doesn't lie because God can't lie. It's clear as a bell in regards to our Mediator to the Father.

I pray for all Catholics who are bound by tradition to set themselves free in a personal relationship with God's Holy Word. The scripture informs all of us, Catholic, Jew, or Gentile, we are all in Christ, priests of a royal priesthood and a Holy nation. I'm not picking on Catholicism. I'm just saying that no man, priest, or prophet can get us into heaven. Any religion, group of people or teachers who offer eternity or salvation without Jesus Christ, the Son of God, as the direct route and the only exclusive way is nothing less than a blind guide leading the blind. *"And if a blind man guides a blind man, both will fall into a pit."* (154)

I love when the Mormon proselytizers come knocking on my door with their false doctrines and the reinstitution of the Aaronic and Levitical priesthoods. I'll fight any cult practitioner with the Sword of the Spirit. I might not be a full-fledged apologist, but I do know how to 'rightly divide the Word of Truth'. The only thing that reinstituted any priesthood in this world was the death and resurrection of One, Jesus Christ of Nazareth; the Son of the Living God and this institution wasn't named after Aaron or Levi. There is only one name under all of heaven and earth by which we find salvation and that name is Jesus Christ. Praise and bless His Holy name!

I'm proud to be a member of the priesthood of all believers. I'm fighting the good fight. I'm going to finish the race set before me. I'm keeping the faith, for "in the future there is laid up for me the crown of righteousness, which the Lord, the righteous judge will award to me on that day; and not only to me, but also to all who have loved His appearing." (155)

I suppose it's only fair that I give some explanation why I appear to attack the Mormon Church. The reason is simple. From its inception, it's been full of fraud, murder and greed. Satan is the father of all lies but the Mormon Church is a close second. If you think our government is good at cover-ups, the Mormons are the masters! How else could it be possible that none of them seem to be aware that the great prophet Brigham Young was a cold-blooded murderer! In 1857 he ordered the assassination of over one hundred innocent men, women and children through one of his brainwashed bishops John D. Lee, just to steal their prized horses, cattle and all their wagons. They took everything these innocent people worked for their whole lives.

Lee confessed and 20 years later was convicted and executed for the "Mountain Meadow Massacre" in Utah. If any Mormon denies this they are one of two things: deceived or a liar. There is plenty of historical proof of this incident. Just do some research. The best author on the subject of cults and religions with corrupt beginnings, without question, is Dr. Walter Martin who wrote 'The Kingdom of the Cults' (revised 1985). This man was never once defeated in any debates (most wouldn't get near him) with cult religious leaders. He challenged many and always brought the darkness into the light. The Mormon Church avoided him like the plague. If you want the facts, read his book. You'll never be the same and you won't believe what the Mormons have done to maintain one of the wealthiest scams and cover-ups on earth!

Neither Joseph Smith, the founder of Mormonism, nor Brigham Young were true prophets of God. Gods test for the true prophet of God is one hundred percent accuracy in fulfillment, all the time in every detail of the prophecy given. Read Deuteronomy 18:20-22. The Mormon Church wins first place among cults in **Revelations of Convenience**. As with the 'Book of Mormon' which if you compare to today's version, there is probably over one thousand changes. My father owns an original copy of the first issue of the 'Book of Mormon' and the difference of today's version says it all. It's not a holy book. It's a record of false prophets wandering minds used to seduce people with lesser intellect or vulnerable behaviors. Every time in Mormon history that the church got in a jam, one of their 'prophets' had a "revelation of convenience" from God no less, to fix the problem. For example: In June 1978 the Mormon Church issued a statement which was a 'divine revelation' from God that now its 'okay' for blacks to be allowed into the priesthood. This was only done because society would no longer put up with this discrimination. Brigham Young (false prophet) clearly stated that Negro's would never hold the priesthood. Now, if he was a prophet, who would dare change that? Another Mormon of course! The same thing happened with polygamy. First, it wasn't okay, then it was, then it wasn't again! Come on people. Let's call a spade a spade! There are so many of these 'revelations of convenience' in the Book of Mormon it's absurd! It's one big scam!

    Remember my book's purpose is to have people understand the dangers of false religions who misuse Gods word for worldly gain. That's the only reason I write about cult religions. Look how easily millions of biblically illiterate people are being misled. Even a guy like Mitt Romney, as smart as he is, never did his research! A perfect example of blind guides leading the blind!

    There is only one more author I must mention and that's Floyd McElveen who wrote 'The Mormon Revelations of Convenience' copyright 1978 - Bethany Fellowship, Inc., Minneapolis, Minnesota. This book makes the Mormon Church's creditability worthless! I understand that this book 'Revelations of Convenience' is no longer in print and may be difficult to find, however, I have two original copies and would send the information, however necessary, to anyone requesting it because the truth must once more be brought into the light. It's been told that when books this dangerous are published, the Mormon Church buys every copy they can to hide the truth from its members.

Well, enough of the cults. It's time to move on! I do hope some of you though, will do some research and help the cause of Christ! Who knows, maybe you will convert a Mormon! Trust me though, it's not easy. They are superbly brainwashed.

If those individuals reading this message want to wear the crown of righteousness, then unchain the Bible from the post of your life, the things that steal your precious devotion time, God's time! Priests and pastors seem to be the only ones reading and expositing the Word to others. Individual Bible dedication today is almost nil. The difference in the amount of time spent watching that idolatrous television and the time devoted to the Bible is astronomical. I won't go any further to avoid causing embarrassment. "The Wheel of Fortune" won't store up for you any treasures in heaven.

People spend more time in the mirror in America, making the exterior look good than they would ever consider reading the Bible. Jesus said a mouthful when he said, "For you clean the outside of the cup and of the dish, but inside you are guilty of robbery and self-indulgence!" (157) It surely can't be much longer before this is found in the dictionary under *American, (Self-Indulgence)*.

Jesus also says, *"For you are like whitewashed tombs which on the outside appear beautiful, but inside you are full of dead men's bones and all uncleanness!"* (157) At the sight of religiosity, Jesus cried out (my paraphrase) *"O my children, my children, how often I wanted to gather you close to Myself, like a hen gathers her chicks under her wing, but you were unwilling. Behold your house is going to be found empty."* (158)

In Jesus' day, the outside of caskets were whitewashed to make them attractive. On the inside there was nothing but death and decay. This picture seems to portray in a morbid way the practices of Christianity today. Plastic Christians break my heart. So do the teachers of their technology. Remember, people, apples don't fall far from the tree. Watered-down, complacent messages don't save souls and convince sinners to repent, but the soul goes home empty, ready for defeat. Have you seen LA preachers yet on TV? Whatever happened to 'Christ must increase and we must decrease'? I guess driving a Rolls Royce is okay when millions are starving every day!

Did Jeremiah or John the Baptist preach peace and prosperity? Prepare ye the way of the coming of the Lord and bring forth fruit in line with repentance, **not your gold collection plates; tithe your life!** God judges wealth in soul value, not dough value. The way some religion is practiced today is the surest way to hell I've ever seen. Need I tell you what the Spirit calls *"pure and undefiled religion in the sight of our God and Father, to visit orphans and widows in their distress and to keep oneself unstained by the world?"* (159)

The purpose of assembling is not to see who on Sunday mornings has on the latest in designer fashions or the nicest double-breasted suit. Real religion is a way of life, not a white cloak to wrap around us on the Sabbath and then cast aside into the six-day closet of unconcern.

I've never known a word to be used more loosely than *Christian*. It carries with it no more reverence and respect than *Bible Banger*. It's becoming a joke, a joke that's fooling no one but the deceived man or woman, the Pharisee, who bears no real Christ-like fruits. It's so meaningless, so uselessly repetitive. I guess Solomon says it best: *"Like a dog that returns to its vomit is a fool who repeats his folly!"* (160) I'm sorry, people, that's the best I can do for the moment.

The lack of true devotion to God's Word can best be illustrated through a true life experience related to me by a true man of God and, without question, a dynamic man of the Word. Believe me, it showed in his preaching. I listened to him in 1986 and I will never forget him or his message. His name is Dr. Ken Chant. His love for God and His word were evident in his eloquent preaching.

As a matter of fact, it was his sermon on the importance of studying God's Word that has left an indelible mark on my soul to this day. His spirit-filled preaching penetrated the innermost part of my being. This was surely what the writer of Hebrews was referring to when he wrote, *"For the Word of God is living and active and sharper than any two-edged sword and PIERCING as far as the division of soul and spirit, of both joints and marrow, and able to judge the thoughts and intentions of the heart."* (161) Hey prosperity preachers; news flash!

You are not fooling anyone who knows Gods word! "The man of the spirit appraises ALL things." Not SOMETHINGS!

I just pray that my straightforward, no-nonsense writing will have the same effect on the readers of this book that this man's preaching had on my soul. If it does and people begin to cherish God's Word again, then I have accomplished what I set out to do in writing this book.

I now want to close this book with a short, but real-life example of the travesty permeating Christian leaders today. I see an epidemic drought; the churches of God today are starving for the Word of God!

The man who spoke at the dedication service for the opening of the new bible college was originally from Australia. He was then living in California and had come to Minnesota to bless the new students and encourage them with a fine message. He was obviously very well respected and well known in Australia because he was asked to be the speaker at a conference in Adelaide, Australia, of 2000 preachers, teachers, and evangelists.

Before he began his message to all the teachers of God's Word, he felt prompted to ask a question which went like this, "Before giving my message, I would like everybody here who has read the entire Bible from front to back, who knows positively that they have read every word in it from Genesis to Revelation to stand up."

He said he wasn't sure of the response he would get, but he was shocked at the one he did get. Later he said to us, "The response was so embarrassing that I was almost tempted to walk off the platform."

Only about 400 people stood up! Now keep in mind that when he came to give his message, he thought he was going to be giving it to Bible-loving preachers, leaders of our Christian faith. When he asked, "How many of those have read it twice, every page, please remain standing," more than half of those standing sat down.

He continued right up to ten readings of the Bible. Only two remained standing—one other person and himself.

My conclusion, brothers and sisters of God, is this, 'many aspire but few attain.' If we take this real-life example seriously and consider the number of people, especially involved as leaders and shepherds of Christianity, who actually devote themselves to the study of Scripture, we should be horrified!

In pondering the words of this great preacher, I am reminded of Jesus in Matthew, chapter 4 when Jesus fought the big battle with Satan in the desert. What saved Him three times in a row? It was the Word of God, directly quoted. Jesus didn't say, "Just a minute, Satan, I need to grab my Bible from the saddlebag on my donkey." Instead, Jesus retorted with a response quoted from God's Holy Word. He had it written on His heart!

Does the reader realize what could have happened if Jesus would have lost that confrontation, if His heart would have been full of other fleshly thoughts or the sole doctrines taught by men on a pedestal?

I'm not so convinced that a lot of Christians today really do know how fortunate we are to have a sinless Savior, one who was so in tune with the Word of God that even under immense pressure, the very first thing which came to His mind was the Word of God. He would never have made it to the cross without that victory. And, of course, without that victory, we would be completely without hope for eternal life.

If the Word of God, the Bible within itself, can do for others what it did to me, which I know it can, then we, as Christ's messengers, have really missed the boat on fulfilling the *Great Commission*. We will have failed to utilize the most powerful tool in the universe to change people's lives, and give them the same opportunity that we freely received; a chance at eternal life and the forgiveness of all our sins.

I write these confident words from harsh, tough experiences. I was dead and brought back to life, abundant life and it didn't happen through a sermon, TV, pastor or bible college. All these can be great, once you have a foundation built on truth. The word of God must always come first. Without this priority reinstated, America is doomed.

How will you claim victory in your "desert temptation" to go out and win souls for Jesus without the WORD OF GOD written on your heart? Please go and share Christ with someone today and give them God's Word, for it is only through this that we can have confidence that we've given them life.

It may well be said that the most dangerous word in the English language is the word "tomorrow". It may be a grim thought, but it is a necessary thought that we have no bond on time. No one knows if for him tomorrow will ever come. There is an old story of three apprentice devils who were coming from Earth to Hell to serve their time. They were telling Satan before they left what they proposed to do. One said, "I will tell men that there is no God." "That," said Satan, "will not do because in their heart of hearts they know there is." "I will tell men," said the second, "that there is no hell." "That," said Satan, "is still more hopeless for even in life they have experienced the remorse of hell." "I will tell men," said the third, "that there is no hurry to change your way of living!" "Go," said Satan, "tell them that and you will ruin them by the millions!!"

Now I would like to leave those people in America, whose lives are bound up deep in the quagmire of materialism, with a sound word of wisdom:

"HOW MUCH BETTER IT IS TO GET WISDOM THAN GOLD! AND TO GET UNDERSTANDING IS TO BE CHOSEN ABOVE SILVER!" (162) CHOOSE YOU THIS DAY WHOM YOU WILL SERVE!

And to all of you who know Christ, I must ask you; when you die, how will your obituary read? Will it simply be a 2"x2" picture listing your immediate family members and a few short paragraphs or will it read like this: Jim lived a lively 89 years. Never did he pass by a hungry or saddened soul. His generosity could not be outdone! If he had his last $10.00 in his pocket, he would try to come up with $11.00 for you! His smile and countenance radiated the love of Christ. Always at the ready to share the love of Christ. It was amazing, even at 89 years old, how people were drawn to his joyful expressions and his thankfulness for all those he met. His humility was unmatched. Whenever he heard others speak unkindly of someone, he was always quick to remind the scoffer, "Remember son, the pancake always has two sides!" Never a harsh word came from his lips, only encouragement. I was with him the day he passed from death onto life! His final words were these: "Take my hand Lord Jesus, I'm coming home!"

Just one last thing I would like to ask all those people reading or listening to this message, especially those who refer to themselves as Christians. If you were put on trial today for being a Christian, would they be able to find enough evidence against you to find you guilty?

He was called by the papacy, "a squabbling monk," a man in whom the fear of God dwelt. This man, who because of his relationship to God and the closeness thereof, was able to see things the vast majority, including those who classified themselves as "Christians," could not. He had *"more insight than all of his teachers!"* (1) *"He understood more than the aged!"* (2) He had "spiritual" eyes, eyes that could see the very heart of God. He had Spiritual ears, ears that heard the still small voice of God speaking through the Holy Spirit, ears that recognized the voice of his Father crying out for the Salvation of the souls of His lost children. He had *"turned his eyes away from looking at vanity"* (3) in order to see reality and he saw it–spiritual reality, the identical reality we are facing today, imminent destruction, slowly and methodically, advancing toward our homeland.

The only difference is that the westward moving, invading Turks under Suleiman, now approaching the borders of Germany in 1526, who inflicted a disastrous defeat upon the Christian army at Mohac's just east of Germany in Hungary, didn't have the catastrophic weaponry available to them as do the enemies of our nation today. In Martin Luther's day, Christians faced a feared and brutal enemy, who like ours today, slaughtering human life without the slightest hesitation. Not only are Christians targeted, we are all targeted.

I have studied the Saint, Martin Luther (1483-1546) extensively. I must clarify at this point, that I do not one hundred percent agree with everything he believed and taught. Martin Luther, like all men, was fallible and prone to times of Spiritual ignorance during Spiritual growth with God. The Apostle Peter would be a good example of this theory. I am, however, in complete agreement with one comment he was said to have made during the period of what seemed to be the inevitable invasion by the barbaric Turks, not to mention the recently signed Treaty of Madrid, on January 14, 1526, which formed a powerful and much feared alliance between Spain and France to Germany's western borders.

It appeared to the Protestant folk that they were being surrounded by unconquerable enemies. It was during this time of great uncertainty and fear of invading enemies closing in on their borders in Germany, when Dr. Martin Luther made the "supposed" following statement: "Why is it that everyone so greatly fears the invasion of the Turks? Should we not all, rather fear the God who's allowing this?"

Here's a man who clearly had keen insight into the consistent character of God in judging sin as clearly seen throughout the entire Old Testament, and he also understood the all-encompassing power and providence of the God who was and is ultimately in control of all human affairs, including war! The prophet Isaiah's words still speak to the heart of the alert saints today: *"Behold, I Myself have created the smith who blows the fire of coals, And brings out a weapon for its work; and I have created the destroyer to ruin!"* (4) King Solomon also gives glory to God in acknowledging God's sovereignty over human affairs when he states, *"The Lord has made EVERYTHING,* (even the Turks, Osama Bin Laden and Isis) *for its own purpose, Even the wicked for the day of evil!"* (5)

It seems clear from Martin's statement that he viewed all circumstances from a Divine perspective. America as a nation would do well to heed this insight, lest it be overcome by forces beyond their control. This includes our military forces. Pride always goes before the fall. In relation to Divine will and power, the United States is far from being a superpower. To the contrary, we are POWERLESS! *"For the Lord of Hosts has planned, and who can frustrate it? And as for His stretched-out hand, who can turn it back?"* (6) The implied answer is obvious–NO ONE! Now some critics may say here that the Old Testament is not applicable to today's issues, but I would tell them that God's immutable or unchangeable character is! And yes, God did make and still does today, EVERYTHING and EVERYONE, to ultimately fulfill His divine plan to judge the Godless and evildoers, not just men, but entire nations!

Martin Luther was not afraid. What purpose would fear of man serve? He feared God, who could *"destroy both the body and the soul in hell!"* (7) Once God has purposed something, especially relating to destruction, there are only two things I believe, and history substantiates these, that can change God's intentions. The first one is intercessory prayer, which I contend has, up to this point, been the only factor in keeping this entire world from complete destruction. The second is repentance. God is patient; beyond our comprehension, but He is also a God of Justice, Judgement, Recompense and Holiness. If you have found and received Christ, you need not fear any judgement!

Anyone who knows God's character, through his Word, knows that God allows only so much iniquity or "self-willed lawlessness" before *"A destruction is determined, overflowing with righteousness!"* (8) What exactly does God mean by "overflowing with righteousness?" I'll tell you what it means. God has waited over 2000 years, has been so patient, so forgiving, so generous and has been so full of undeserved favor and prosperity with this sinful and idolatrous nation that the evidence against the Godless, without Christ, is overwhelming. There is no room left for argument or excuse! Without true repentance, like that of King David, who himself was a murderer and adulterer, as recorded in Psalm 51, without an admission from a "broken and contrite heart," without this personal action, individually and together as a nation, the destruction of America is imminent. As are all other nations!

It simply saddens me to see the overwhelming fear that the falling of the Twin Towers in New York City has caused worldwide. People must understand that this was nothing less than a warning, not only to America as a nation, but to all the nations of the world. It's no different than when God's instrument of destruction, the nation Assyria, crushed the Northern Kingdom of Israel while Judah stood by and watched. God purposed this specifically to urge Judah, the Southern Kingdom, to repent. Now let me be clear here. God didn't do it, He allowed it!

The annihilation of America's greatest symbol of prosperity, its pride and symbol of achievement, came down in a horrific display of power beyond our ability to control. No evil in this world is allowed without Almighty God's consent! The devil, asking God's permission to crush his servant Job, substantiates my claim. God plainly allowed this to happen. To believe otherwise is simply ignorance of God's sovereignty and, therefore, fruitless, in regards to making the changes "Spiritually" America needs so desperately.

Terrorists are nothing less than instruments of God's wrath, a rod of destruction wielded by the God of Recompense, (Jehovah El Gmolah). Read the books of Isaiah and Jeremiah. Why did God allow the Assyrian and Babylonian captivities of His children, many of whom were killed in the process?

Nebuchadnezzar, King of Babylon, was nothing but a puppet in the hand of God. Cyrus, who released God's children to return to their homeland after seventy years of foretold captivity, was also the same.

Consider also Pharaoh in Egypt before the Great Exodus. God gave him his life and his position for only one reason—that God and His great power might be made known to all nations! God allowed numerous lives to be taken, which today might be considered innocent lives, just to serve his own Holy and Righteous purposes. Many more have died since in Spain, Iraq, Africa, Israel, Palestine, Afghanistan, and many other numerous places worldwide, including innocent Americans! It's hard to even count the number of men, women and children murdered in cold blood in Syria under Assad's reign!

As I am writing these words, many evil, depraved minds are planning their next acts of terrorism against the United States and anyone else who appears to be our ally. When and where shall they strike next? When Luther spoke of the Devil's hatred and power, he said, "On earth is not his equal!" Anyone who dismisses these words is in very grave danger. When the world is taken over by gangs, cartels and terrorists, eventually there will be no place left to hide. We couldn't win against Vietnam's guerrilla-style warfare, nor can we win a war against suicidal terrorists! God, however, can! You know the world is a dangerous place when, for instance, children in Palestine now have a new game, in which they collect and trade "Palestinian Martyr Cards!"

If things don't change, destruction is imminent. Do you hear me??!! The simplicity of the words of the great American abolitionist, Sojourner Truth (1797-1883) would fit America's present danger and impending doom: "You may hiss as much as you'd like, but it's comin'."

Many people today prefer not to know the blatant truth of their present situation, so as to go about their daily routine unhindered and continue to seek and find their own desires. Americans have clearly accomplished finding their own Godless desires! I must inform the reader at this point that my calling is not (unlike many others) to speak popular truths, but to speak the truth, period!

I make no apologies for my vociferous style of writing or speaking. I make no claims of superior righteousness, other than Christ's. I don't care what people say about me personally. I care only that people come to know the truth of Christ and His sacrificial death and resurrection and His willingness to receive all who come to him with a pure repentant heart for the salvation of their souls! Even many churches today, especially the larger ones, have lost their focus. They spend more time running the business of church then focusing on doing God's business! The gold value outshines the soul value!

America went wrong when it strayed from Christ. At the time of the American War for Independence, 98.4% of Americans were Protestant, 1.4% were Catholic and .15% were Jewish. The American population was 99.8% Christian! Clearly, these numbers have gone consistently downward and they show the weakness of the present foundation upon which America is built. Any good architect knows what happens to things built on weak foundations. The tiniest earthquake will damage the structure. Right now, we can feel the quaking in America and around the globe. Anyone who denies the danger is simply blind.

America was given independence for God's glory and to propagate the Good News. Americans now use their independence to do what is right in their own eyes. The entire book of Judges tells of a stubborn and rebellious people just like today's America. Everyone is doing just as they please without the slightest respect for God and His purposes. Look what's happened to God's institution of marriage? Living in sin isn't living in sin anymore. People don't realize that God is still on His throne watching! We've truly lost our independence and are now a nation in slavery to sin and uncleanliness.

John Adams, President of our once great nation said, "The general principles on which the fathers achieved independence are the general principles of Christianity. *(Notice, it doesn't say Islam!)* I will now avow that I then believe and now believe that those general principles of Christianity are as Eternal and Immutable as the attributes and characteristics of God!" This statement here also confirms what I stated earlier that God's character is always the same! America is desperately in need of some serious Spiritual introspection.

I would like at this point to direct the reader's attention to the words of the prophet Jeremiah, taken from the book of Lamentations. I want the reader to see the similarities between the desolation of Jerusalem in 586 B.C. and what Jeremiah Spiritually saw as the reasons for this act of God and how sovereign God was in the whole affair and how astoundingly these 2,590-year-old words fit America's situation today in relation to what ***I know*** is again the judgement of God falling upon a sinful, idolatrous nation.

The theme of the book of Lamentations, "Woe to us for we have sinned," fits America quite snugly. The very first verse, *"How lonely sits the city,"* (9) speaks volumes in relation to the hearts of Godless men and women today. Loneliness is one of the first signs representative of a person without Christ. God allows this as a way to draw people to Him, yet how many of us look everywhere else except to Christ for comfort and consolation during times of loneliness and emptiness? We use drugs, psychiatrists, mediums, counselors with no spiritual life themselves, alcohol, sex, suicide, the list goes on! Oh yes, and don't forget the positive thinking seminars and preachers!

Jeremiah goes on to say that the nation *"has none to comfort her."* *"All her friends* (like some of our allies in war) *have dealt treacherously with her."* (10) They abandoned her. *"All her pursuers have overtaken her in the midst of distress."* (11) *"Her enemies* (our terrorists) *prosper."* Why? *"For the Lord, (not the enemy) has caused her grief because of her transgressions."* (12) Only God can count high enough to count America's transgressions. *"All who honored her despise her."* (13) This sounds to me just like the attitude of the United Nations and others who don't want to get involved in our huge mess.

The next verse is sure to hit home with those who have ignored God's sovereignty and mandates. *"She did not consider her future; therefore, she has fallen astonishingly."* (14) *"For the enemy has magnified himself!"* (14) *"The adversary* (radical Islam physically and nonviolent Islam spiritually) *has stretched out his hand over all her precious things!"* (15) It's evident what's being destroyed physically in the United States and elsewhere, but the seemingly overlooked threat of the religion of Islam itself is a TREMENDOUS 'spiritual' danger! Any religion, which doesn't teach Jesus Christ as the risen Son of God, and equal with the Father is a threat to Christianity and a danger to the world. This threat must be fought by Christians, not with the physical sword, but with the Word of God 'spoken' in the Spirit.

It is America's complacency with regards to idolatrous religions that is stirring up the wrath of God. God's warning to the children of Israel before entering the Promised Land is a clear indication of where we've gone wrong as a nation by allowing the infiltration of idolatry into our land. The Apostle Paul in his letter to the Galatians makes crystal-clear what our position is to be on the issue. *"But even though we, 'or any Angel from heaven'* (This alone makes a tolerance for Islam or any Spiritless religion a violation of God's commands) *should preach to you a gospel contrary to that which we have preached to you* (Christ as Savior by Faith alone) *let him be accursed! As we have said before, so I say again now* (Paul repeating himself twice should make evident that this issue is a very, very serious issue) *if 'any' man* (Muslim, Mormon, Jehovah's Witness, Buddhist, Kabbalist, Christian Scientist, Hindu, the list is endless) *is preaching to you a gospel contrary to that which you received, let him be accursed!"* (16)

I must now explain the word, *accursed,* since the majority of Christians in America obviously don't understand its importance to God, our Father and the Lord Jesus Christ. The original Greek word for "accursed" is *anathema*. It specifically denotes a religious ban or an excommunicated thing or person. Thus, it means, "to bind under a great curse." *Anathema* as a noun is translated from Greek to mean "a thing devoted to God for destruction. This could be an idol, a city, a person, or a group of persons causing the disfavor of God. The word in Galatians 1:8-9 stresses that which is dedicated not to God's honor but to its own destruction. (Strongs Concordance)

So many Christians don't even see this spiritual warfare! If you don't believe Islam, the religion itself, not the people per-say are dangerous; you don't have a clue about God's hatred of Idolatry! Most don't want to know these truths! St. Augustine called these types; "Blind & Pigheaded!" I call them oblivious to truth and in for a rude and deadly awakening!! "Have we verbally or otherwise instituted a religious ban on those religions which cause the disfavor of God?" The answer is clearly NO! Have we as a nation incurred the disfavor of God? Yes, unequivocally, yes.

America is littered with idolatrous and blasphemous religions. King Solomon's Spiritual demise was from nothing less than trying to please his foreign wives, who demanded access to worship foreign gods. This affected his relationship with the One and only true God, the Father of our Lord Jesus Christ. If only today Christians had the zeal and devotion toward our Lord and Savior that the Muslims have toward their God Allah. American worshipers' hearts are divided. The desires of the flesh have destroyed allegiance and true, wholehearted worship.

If only every Christian could witness what I experienced once in a church full of approximately 250 Haitian Christians. These were people whose lives knew nothing but poverty. I have never once in my life in any church in America seen such tremendous freedom and power in worship. God Himself inhabited the praises of His people that day. Never have I been so frozen in awe by the presence of God! I literally was unable to move my body. I trembled with a reverent fear and an unexplainable feeling of unworthiness to be even near the God, my Lord, whose presence filled the room. On this day, I was profoundly changed by revelation, never to be the same man again.

It's very interesting to watch Americans, the majority of whom rarely ever take time to talk with and get to know strangers, let alone ever reach out and help someone, until disaster strikes. It's simply amazing how people during times like this become completely different people. Their reaction is only natural and godly, yet without destruction, people show how unnatural and how ungodly we as a nation and as a people have become. Is it any wonder that God must go to such catastrophic measures to wake up America, the Spiritual sleeping giant? Historically, God has not changed his methods. Since America was founded, only its people have changed. Materialism and perverted social media have had a huge hand in misguiding our desires and complacency to sin. Parents that both work and place more emphasis on money and bigger houses than their kids' morality have clearly destroyed the futures of this generation and the rest that shall follow!

Now, to continue on with Jeremiah's relevant Lamentations, chapter 1:14 continues to show God's sovereignty in human affairs when Jeremiah states, *"He has made my strength fail; the Lord has given me into the hands of those against whom I am not able to stand.*" (17) *"The Lord has rejected all my strong men* (Henceforth, our inability to halt terrorism). *God has called an appointed time against me to crush my young men!"* (18) We seem to be losing a lot of young men in uniform today. *"My children are desolate because the enemy has prevailed!"* (19) We must acknowledge the fact America, that our present situation is nothing less than an "appointed time." Verse 17 is one in which I want the reader to pay close attention to *"The Lord has COMMANDED concerning Jacob,* (Today we are Jacob) *that the ones around him should be his adversaries."* (20)

It's quite simple, folks; God has commanded our present situations in order to bring about repentance. Verse 2 of chapter 2 also has an interesting reference to our present situation: *"How the Lord has covered the daughter of Zion with a cloud in His anger!"* (21) This cloud represents darkness and confusion. It's hard to function and be successful or productive in the dark, isn't it? The cloud also signifies a disadvantage.

Without question, the types of warfare America is involved in today and the nature and geographical situation it is facing are factors in our military's inability to use its full power and technology in a conventional war. Our present enemy is far more complex than anything we ever faced in Vietnam. Our new enemy could be your local baker, shop owner, auto mechanic, stockbroker, doctor and even college students!

Don't be deceived by the information in the media. We, as a nation, are in grave imminent danger, both physically and, more importantly, Spiritually. The Spiritual aspect carries with it ETERNAL RAMIFICATIONS. The other does not. Towers and trains and buses can be replaced quite easily, but let's see anyone on this earth replace a dead, 'lost', human soul. The wealthy people who have had their bodies frozen after death with the hopes of being given another shot at life are going to be more than disappointed. It's people who do these types of ridiculous things that should be a sign to all who live and breathe how empty Spiritually America is as a nation. Also, if I may add here, Isis is not 'under control' and 'on the run' as our government would like you to believe. It's spreading like the fires of Hell!

Chapter 2:5 says, *"The Lord has become like an enemy. He has swallowed up Israel.* (22) The only comment necessary regarding this verse is that the last enemy on earth a nation wants is God! Good luck—you'll need it! God's wars are orchestrated in the heavens far beyond our military's capabilities.

Later in chapter 2:13-14, the Prophet cries out to a broken and astonished people who have been silenced and humiliated by God's awesome show of power: *"Who can heal you?"* Implying no one, He continues, *"Your prophets have seen for you false and foolish visions and they have not exposed your iniquity, so as to restore you from captivity."* (23) These words are a stunningly accurate depiction of the compromise and complacency we see from preachers in the pulpits of the churches in America today. The majority of preachers, pastors and teachers have utterly failed at being bold and concise in their attack against sin and worldliness, homosexuality, gay and lesbian marriages, civil unions, trash on the media, promiscuity, lust and greed and a host of sinful influences which attack not only Christ but all the rest of the lost souls Christ grieves over! America is bound in captivity by the cords of their sin. *"Do not be deceived, God is not mocked, for whatever a man sows, this he will also reap."* (24)

Satan is slowly using his influences of worldly pleasure to infiltrate and corrupt the hearts and minds of God's people so subtly that it's getting more difficult each day to notice any real difference between a Christian and a heathen. The Light of Christ is slowly and deceptively being snuffed out by the enemy. Only sin is to be blamed. Truly, all of Christianity today suffers from a lack of a real understanding of the Holiness of our God and Savior, the Lord Jesus Christ. Imagine, for example, the hatred or disdain people feel when they see on the news a story of a grown man who repeatedly raped a four-year-old girl. Most of us become livid with anger–it burns! Well, multiply that (hatred) by one million. This is as close as I can come to comprehending God's hatred for sin (not the sinner, the sin itself). This is exactly why God sent His son! It is our sin, past, present and future, that Christ died for; was tortured for to set us free!

I will now continue with three verses of chapter 2, which need no explanation, whatsoever. Consider America's present war with Islamic terrorists as you read the following words. I will leave the reader to interpret for themselves. *"They hiss and shake their heads* (a sign of disdain and disrespect) *at the daughter of Jerusalem.* (God's people today) *Is this the city of which they said, the perfection of beauty,* (America) *a joy to all the earth? All the enemies have opened their mouths against you; they hiss and gnash their teeth. They say, "We have swallowed her up! Surely this is the day for which we waited; we have reached it, we have seen it."* (25) *"The Lord has done what He proposed. He has accomplished His word. He has thrown down without sparing and He has caused the enemy to rejoice over you. He has exalted the might of your adversaries!"* (25) The spiritual blindness of our world leaders today astounds me! For example: Trying to buy peace with Iran for hundreds of millions of dollars and removal of old sanctions! What human with half a brain would do this! Iran has lied to us so many times it's ridiculous! This is a battle between good and evil! Listen carefully. 'The weapons of our warfare are **NOT CARNAL**, but mighty in the spirit for the destruction of fortresses! Without divine intervention, our gooses are cooked, literally! Back to Jeremiah!

Now that I've hopefully convinced the reader of the relevance of Jeremiah's words in relation to our present situation (We are after all dealing with the same God), I would like to interject here the available hope that the discouraged prophet Jeremiah also saw, even amidst this terrible destruction. It's the exact same hope that we as a nation may still have available if it's not too late to sway the destroying arm of the Lord. I personally believe there is still some time, but not very much, of that I'm quite confident! Let me put it this way. I wouldn't want to be unsaved and find out it's too late! Please let the reader allow the following words to bring hope!

(Lamentations 3:20-40) *The Lord's lovingkindness indeed never cease. For His compassions never fail. They are new every morning; great is Thy faithfulness. The Lord is good to those who wait for Him. To the person who seeks Him.* (It is noteworthy to mention here that many of God's promises and blessings are contingent on actions initiated by ourselves. Often when an individual exhibits an act of trust or faith in God, this is the moment in which the arm of God's protection moves earthward on one's behalf. Abraham's attempt to sacrifice (kill) his son was stopped by an Angel of God in answer to the faithful actions exhibited by Abraham.

It is good that he waits silently for the salvation of the Lord.

It is good for a man that he should bear the yoke in his youth. (The yoke of correction)

Let him (the sinner) *sit alone and be silent,* (humble) *since He* (God) *has laid it on him.* (The afflictions)

Let him put his mouth in the dust, (a sign of surrender) *perhaps there is hope.*

Let him give his cheek to the smiter; (accept the discipline, regardless of the instrument God has chosen) *let him be filled with reproach.*

For the Lord will not reject forever.

For if He causes grief, then He will have compassion, according to His lovingkindness.

For He does not afflict willingly, or grieve the sons of men. (Everything God does is based on love and righteousness.)

To crush under His feet all the prisoners of the land, to deprive a man of justice in the presence of the Most High,

To defraud a man in his lawsuit, of these things the Lord does not approve.

'Who is there who speaks and it comes to pass unless the Lord has commanded it?' (This statement is the epitome of power!)

Is it not from the mouth of the Most high that both good and ill go forth? The implied answer here is, 'of course'!

Why should any living mortal, or any man, offer complaint in view of his sins? (With these words in mind, America should remain silent!)

Let us examine and probe our ways, and let us return to the Lord! (26) (If America only heeded this one Holy Word of God, the Lord's anger may be calmed!) These words from Jeremiah are truly my cry and objective of this entire book. Contemplate our spiritual reality and return to the Lord!

What the reader just read is a beautiful synopsis of God's character, His love, His ways, His purposes, His objectives and certainly His all-encompassing control over all human affairs! Truly, not even a single sparrow falls to the ground without the Father knowing!

Now since I'm on the subject of the words of the prophets relating to our present situation in America, especially spiritually, I want to briefly touch on a few words of Isaiah from Chapter 6, when God called Isaiah to speak to His wayward children, who refused to repent, just prior to their deportation of 70 years in captivity in Babylon. God had warned them repeatedly, to no avail. The following words of Isaiah 6:9-10 were also reiterated by the Apostle Paul in Rome to self-righteous, hard-hearted people. I now reiterate them to those "religious" people of America today, still "playing church"! These words of Isaiah are quoted repeatedly as applicable also to New Testament times! We today live in a troubled world. Material prosperity and comforting innovations have brought America down to its knees into tragic Spiritual decline! The people have forsaken God and his ways of righteousness. Social and moral conditions today are the spitting image of Israel and Judah before God unleashed His wrath and judgement. The rich keep getting richer and the poor become poorer. As in Isaiah's day, so is it today that people are clinging to the external forms of religion, but the vast majority truly knows nothing of Christ's true meaning and His power. As I stated from Lamentations, God loves His people. He's always ready to forgive a sinner, but the fact remains, the most important fact America has seemingly forgotten, that God is bound by His own Holiness and Righteousness and consistent character, to judge all those who continue on in their evil ways.

Pay close attention to Isaiah's words, which went unheeded by a nation spiritually like ours before they reaped judgement. These words are truly of us today: And he said, *"Go and tell this people: keep on listening but do not perceive: keep on looking but do not understand. Render the hearts of this people insensitive, their ears dull and their eyes dim,* (America's spiritual perception has become so dull that up to the falling of the Twin Towers, we as a nation have still failed to heed even the most severe warnings coming down out of heaven) *lest they see with their eyes, hear with their ears, understand with their hearts and return to be healed!"* (27)

I must say too, like Pharaoh who refused to comply with God's warnings, we too are refusing to comply. The only difference is that it's not God who has hardened our hearts. We have brought this situation upon ourselves by rejecting repeated warnings from God, given through word and circumstance. The Spiritual phenomenon which has made us blind to God's warnings and truths is explained quite easily by any God-fearing, Bible-loving man or woman of God. Very simply, every time we reject or ignore the truth from a Biblical perspective, our hearts become harder and harder and our Spiritual perceptions (if we have any in the first place) become dull until eventually, we lose all ability to discern any real Spiritual perceptions or truth. God is allowing us to destroy ourselves in many ways also. We as a people and nation must fight back Spiritually, stop all complacency and compromise and move out of the darkness back into God's Spiritual light, true reality–God's, not ours!

The Apostle Paul wrote and recorded much of his revelations from God while a prisoner. Much of our New Testament came from a man who once condoned the murder of Christians until he saw the Light, a great Light of Truth, which left him temporarily blind. Christ himself called Paul out of the darkness and into His Marvelous Light. The Lord has done the same for me. This entire book is nothing less than revelations I received from God over a period of twenty-eight years in and out of prison, jails, reform schools and the like. I found the Word of God at age fourteen in the Minnesota State Reformatory at Red Wing, Minnesota, and haven't been able to put it down since. The words you read are not of the flesh but of the Spirit. I was just a man with many defilements of the flesh until *"He who began a good work in me was faithful to complete it!"* (28)

Tribulation has always marked the trail of the true reformer. It was true in the story Paul, Luther, Savonarola, Knox, Wesley and the rest of God's mighty army. They came through great tribulation to their point of power.

Every great book has been written with the author's blood. Who wrote the timeless dream of 'A Pilgrim's Progress'? Was it a prince in royal robes on a couch of comfort and ease? No! The lingering splendor of John Bunyan's vision gilded the dingy walls of an old English prison for twelve years for preaching the Gospel, while he a glorious genius in that environment recorded for us under the guidance of the Holy Spirit, the 2nd most widely read Christian book in the world; 2nd only to the Bible itself!

I would list my sins and evil deeds for the reader, but this would constitute another entire book, more likely a twelve-volume set or something. All I can say is similar to what the blind man healed by Christ said, *"I was blind, now I see!"* (29) I give God all the praise; the honor and the glory due to Him for saving a terrible lost and sinful wretch like me.

I could easily have taken up a comfortable residence in Sodom or Gomorrah at one point in my life. But I've found my Daily Bread and it's been my diet ever since. I wonder if Mr. Atkins found it before he died. I guess we'll find out in heaven, won't we? (At least the few who are going) Always remember, folks, *"The gates to hell are wide and broad is the road which leads to destruction."* (30) Hell needs no reservations. They don't turn people away there either. There's room enough for the entire world's population and then some. The Word of God is quite clear on this issue.

If you don't believe in hell, rest assured, you've got your spot already assigned, unless you find Christ and then, as a result, surrender to Him wholly and without looking back. An old relation of mine from Sodom looked back and that's where she took her last breath. Hell has a voracious appetite for human souls. It's insatiable and it won't change until Christ returns. Be ready!

During my time of imprisonment, I wasted not one hour of one day over an eight-year period. I sought God wholeheartedly and not only did I receive a multitude of Spiritual gifts, I was also honored by God in seeing many souls come to Christ. I still get calls today from people I shared Christ with many years ago. Murderers and every type of sinner imaginable now share in the same freedom and liberty I do today. I once handed out over 400 Bibles during an eight-month stay in a workhouse. Why? Because I knew Christ was the only hope for these individuals, as He is for all peoples and nations. Even Spiritually dead Muslims came alive in Christ!

Islam is the fastest growing religion in the world today and the biggest threat to Christianity. Christians don't want to get involved with this issue. They're afraid and mostly Biblically illiterate. Their illiteracy, Biblically, is surely their biggest downfall. It is America's biggest also. No one could ever debate me on this issue and win. NO ONE! The Word of God is the one and only effective weapon we have against our present situation in America today. Other tactics are one hundred percent useless. As Luther said in his song, "A Mighty Fortress," "That Word above all earthly powers, no thanks to them abideth!"

I should probably interject here that I'm not a Lutheran. I was raised in the Lutheran church, however, but I learned very little. Liturgies and traditions might bring comfort to a worshiper because of their consistency and familiarity, but they do little, if anything, in the transforming of souls. The Catholic Church and many others, in my mind, are wasting a lot of precious time. Any enlightened Christian also knows that denominations are nothing but a separating of the Body of Christ. We all need to be members of a body of believers, and in our search for this, we should use caution; however, an individual is wrong if he continues to avoid fellowship because he can't seem to find the right church. That search could go on into eternity.

Find a good church (the best you can) and support it and become active as a generous giver and as a participant in the reformation of issues that don't line up with God's purposes. Just leaving the church resolves nothing! I wish I had a nickel for every person who left a church in America in the last five years. I would be rich. The words of Paul to Timothy in II Timothy 4:3 are prophetic: *"For the time will come when they will not endure sound doctrine;* (That time is here.) *but wanting to have their ears tickled* (complacency), *they will accumulate for themselves teachers <u>in accordance to their own desires</u>, and will turn aside to myths!"* (31) e.g. homosexuals worshipping in churches that condone their behavior, allowing them to preach from the pulpit while living in blatant sin! I'm speechless!! These prophetic words have been fulfilled. Paul was not designated as a prophet, although many of his words are prophetic in nature. Amos, as based on his own words in Amos 7:14-15, was not a prophet either. Yet God commanded him to go and prophesy. Let me paraphrase his words: "I am not a prophet nor the son of a prophet, but the Lord said unto me, go, prophesy unto my people."

I don't claim to be a prophet. God, however, has clearly directed me to boldly proclaim to His people that which lies within His heart for today. Some call this a forth-telling prophet. I call it a sinner who was saved and filled himself with so much of God's word that he cannot help but proclaim God's truths lest he explodes! I speak unhindered with all openness. *"For I am not ashamed of the Gospel* (nor its consequences), *for it is the power of God for salvation to everyone who believes!"* (32)

The message I've been called to speak is not going to make me any friends among many other religious groups, as you will soon see. I have not the slightest reservation in writing what you're about to read. It's long overdue!

An author named Salman Rushdie wrote the book titled 'The Satanic Verses' published on September 26, 1988. A million-dollar bounty was placed on his head. Maybe mine will be two million? At the direct order of Khomeini, The Death Squads (Radicals) were on the hunt! Just before the Fatwa, Rushdie had written: "A powerful tribe of clerics has taken over Islam. These are the contemporary 'Thought Police'." Every religion has some radical people involved, but when murder is the solution to silence your critics, your holy influence has just been made null and void!

Christians make up approximately thirty-two percent of worldwide religions; Muslims approximately twenty-three percent, Hindus fifteen percent. If Islam rises another nine percent percent and we continue to decline, as I believe we are, what then? Everyone knows there is power in numbers! Religions whose holy books include the Koran of Islam, *the Book of Mormon,* the six volumes of the Jehovah Witnesses' *Scripture Studies* and their *Watch Tower,* which circulates approximately 46 million copies monthly, the Hindus Veda, *Upanishads, Mahabharata and Bhagavad Gita* and the Buddhists' *Tripitaka,* are nothing less than written guides to an eternity of torment and a danger to the naïve! Why? Because they are all missing one element: That Jesus Christ died on the cross, once for all sinners.

The true and only Word of God, the Christian Canon, contains the sixty-six books; thirty-nine in the Old Testament and twenty-seven in the New Testament, is the number one in authority and has never changed since its first writing, unlike many others. Decades of research and facts prove the Bible surpasses all in authenticity! The Mormons, Jehovah Witnesses, Muslims and many others, all used their own variations of Scripture for monetary gain, sexual gratification, and to gain control of others. During my years of incarceration, I've read and studied thousands of pages of literature from St. Thomas Aquinas to Flavius Josephus, Saint Augustine to Muhammad, Tolstoy, Watchman Nee to Plato & Jerome. I've read all major religions and their histories. Most importantly, who the founders were and what type of unholy scandalous pasts they had! If only the young Mormons truly knew their history (and didn't deny it) half their membership would resign tomorrow! They are brainwashed from inception to run from facts. No wonder the Mormon Church is one of the wealthiest institutions on earth! I've studied almost all of Martin Luther's works, some of Will Durant's II volume set 'The History of Civilization', most all the early church fathers, the three-volume set by 'Nobel Prize in Literature' winner Alexander Isayevich Solzhenitsyn (1970), Templeton Prize (1983) Laureate of the International Botev Prize (2008) with his concise history of Russia and 'The Gulag's or Prisons of Russia', under Stalin where millions were murdered. I've read almost every type of religious history and history of the nation's rulers because I wanted a good understanding of both how Godly people can be and how evil people can be! Stalin and Hitler are good examples of the latter. As far as misleading people through false hopes, guys like Joseph Smith and Brigham Young have done immense damage also, especially when you look at the numbers of deceived Mormons and the false hope both they and their children are believing! Cults are an epidemic! You may think I repeat myself a lot, but I make no apologies! These issues have ETERNAL significance! Just count them all as souls lost!

If you want to see how dangerous cults are, just read how on September 11, 1857, a Mormon leader led other Mormon's in the Mountain Meadow Massacre in the execution of approximately 120 innocent men, women and children in Utah. This should open your eyes to the danger of cults, and how weak-minded people are misled to do horrifying, Ungodly acts; just like the young boys who become terrorists today. Later in my book, there are more facts on this!

Without Christ, no one comes to the Father of Abraham, Isaac and Jacob. *"There is only one mediator between God and man and that is the Lord Jesus Christ."* (34) He is Savior and creator of the universe and all it contains. Anyone teaching contrary to these truths is deceived and is a servant of the father of all lies, Satan himself. Such men are instruments and vessels of unrighteousness, in need of Salvation through Christ.

Islam for example, is a religious, social and political danger to every American and Christian believer. Christianity was founded by our risen, 'living', breathing Savior, Jesus Christ. Christ lives today, seated today at the right hand of God the Father in heaven, and so does His Word. Muhammad is dead forever.

The word, *Islam,* means "surrender." Islamists have not, however, surrendered to Christ for salvation. Christian complacency is partially to blame. *The Koran* is the byproduct of a self-proclaimed prophet who plagiarized the Bible and added revelations of convenience and then proclaimed the Koran as the final word of God. It simply is not. The very fact that Christ lives nullifies the possibility that any book including *The Koran* could be authoritative. Muhammad came along five and a half centuries after Christ had risen from the dead, and now Muslims consider him God's final prophet. This is nonsense. Muslims claim that those who follow and obey Allah and Muhammad will go to heaven or paradise.

In the doctrines of Islam, Muslims learn in their *Five articles of Faith* that Allah is not personally knowable. Now combine this with a dead prophet one is supposed to follow to reach paradise, and I see a very hopeless case. Yet Satan has done a great job of blinding millions with falsehoods. Marriage is a requirement for every Muslim, yet in their supposed "holy" book in Sura 4:31, it speaks of a man's right to dominate his wife's behavior, "As for those from whom you fear disobedience, admonish them and banish them to beds apart and hit them!"

So much for a holy book. *The Koran* is truly nothing more than a partial plagiarism of the Bible with many recorded sayings of a man, not a prophet, within its pages. It's really no different than what other cult religions have done by taking the parts of Holy Scripture they need to fit their revelations and build a religion of blind, hungry followers. From a Theological standpoint, Islam is not a cult but has many similarities.

Joseph Smith of the Mormons, Charles Taze Russell of the Jehovah's Witnesses and Muhammad of the Islamic religion all fall into the same category. They are all false prophets, worshipped under Satanic, false spiritual influences, who are followed by unfortunate, spiritually weak individuals looking for hope.

Any book or persons, Angel or institution, tract or teacher, TV program or holy man which preaches to you anything other than that Christ is the risen savior and only through Him can we receive eternal life, not by good works but through faith in Him, is simply man-made, *"earthly, natural and demonic"* (33) and its origins are most positively of the flesh!

It is quite simple, people, Jesus Christ was a sinless prophet and He was also what He claimed to be, the only Son of God. Jesus Christ was then and still is today, (because he is risen) God Himself, equal and one with the Father. Christ was God the Father incarnate, who came to set us free from the curse – ourselves.

Muslims believe that anything Muhammad recorded in the Koran/Quran has authority over any passages in the Bible (finished in 90 a.d.) that doesn't agree with their beliefs. Remember now dear readers, Muhammad wasn't even born until 570 a.d. You do the math!

People think Islam is compatible with Christianity but it's not. They deny the Trinity and the fact that Jesus is one with the Father. He also is not the Son of God either! In their eyes, He was just a prophet, period! Islam is based on works (Kismet). Christianity is based on grace and forgiveness through faith. Christians don't believe in Jihad either! If any readers have any question about the authority of the Bible vs. any holy books, just do some research on the authority of the Holy Bible and you'll see what I mean. There is irrefutable evidence when you measure them all up together. How can one know how long something is without measuring first? I've done the measuring and research.

Let us be clear. *The Koran, The Book of Mormon* and all of the Jehovah's Witnesses' literature and all others which contradict Holy Scripture have no more value in giving eternal life than the paper they are printed on. It wouldn't surprise me if God the Father and the Lord Jesus Christ used all those books to kindle the fires of hell, where all those who teach salvation without Christ are guaranteed to go. It's an eternal guarantee too. No arguments, no paperwork to show, no lawyers, no "Dream Team" to plead your innocence, no last-minute phone calls, no bail bondsmen, nothing!

Not all of Bill Gates' billions could save a soul who meets His creator without Christ's blood covering his sins on the Day of Judgement. It is, therefore, important for Christians to remember the words of Paul to the church in Rome in chapter 10:13-14, *"For whoever will call upon the name of Lord will be saved. How then shall they call upon Him in whom they have not heard? And how shall they hear without a preacher?"* (35) Paul's words are truth, are they not? Of course, they are. They are inspired by God himself. Therefore, based on that truth, the rest of the truth must be told. Notice the words again, "How shall they hear without a preacher?" Remember Christians, we are all members of the priesthood of all believers.

Boldness in sharing Christ openly today is far from meeting the commands and requirements of Scripture. Boldness and fearlessness are almost non-existent in relation to the number of people who call themselves Christians. Why is it also true that very few fear the growing size of false religions growing in America today? I'll tell you why. Only the true Spirit of Christ rebukes falsity, that which opposes God's truth and plan. This Spirit only comes from one place, the Word of God. Remember, you can't love God if you don't love His Word. God and His Word are one and the same. (John 1:1)

Another issue which needs clarifying is that just because you spend a lot of time in Church doesn't make you a Christian. Just because you spend a lot of time in the garage, doesn't make you a car, does it? "Faith without works is dead!" Being good doesn't transform people. God's Word transforms people. The Holy Spirit transforms people. A person's boldness for Christ relates directly to his or her level of love for and commitment to the Word of God and fellowship with Him. It is the Word of God, which is living and active and sharper than any two-edged sword.

The power of Christian work and conversion of lost souls lies in His Word. Read Psalm 119. This says it all! Christ fought Satan in Matthew chapter 4 with the Word written on His heart and defeated Satan's attempt to deceive, and, therefore, defeated Satan's purpose.

Satan is, however, defeating the propagation of the Gospel in America today because of our lack of devotion to God's Word individually. There are, for example, many non-violent sects of Islam. Does that mean that these sects are not a threat to Christianity? Of course not. Just because one's religion or practice thereof causes no physical damage to people doesn't negate its danger. Spiritual dangers are much more to be feared than physical danger.

Jesus said, *"The Kingdom of heaven suffers violence and violent men take it by force."* (36) Many theologians have varied ideas on what this means. My thought is that since *"Our struggle is not against flesh and blood"* (37) and *"The weapons of our warfare are not of the flesh or carnal,"* (38) then I would suggest that these words of Christ refer to the seeming "violence" of opposing Spirits that are fighting constantly for souls. These souls will go to heaven or to hell. There is a last day and the devil knows it, so every day is valuable in our effort to win souls for the Father.

I believe the overwhelming numbers of non-Christian religions, whose forces, unseen at times, are causing enormous battles between good and evil, truth and falsity, in the heavens.

The problem, however, is that only Spiritual eyes, which America lacks today in both the pew and the pulpit, can actually discern and, therefore, fight back with weapons of the Spirit, mainly, *"handling accurately the Word of truth."* (39). The scripture tells us to "Study to show yourself approved unto God."

In regard to physical attacks, as seen the world over today, one must remember a dead body can be raised again through Christ, no problem! On the other hand, though, we would do well to heed the Scriptures' warning, "He who has found his life shall lose it, (lived his years out without acknowledging Christ) (living for themselves a hedonistic lifestyle) and he who has lost his life for My sake shall find it." (40). Sacrificing our desires for His! Those who have made God's purposes here on earth their first priority shall have life and that life shall be eternal.

Now losing one's life eternally, that is a problem! Anyone, who teaches eternal life in heaven or paradise without Christ as the way, is far more dangerous than any suicide bomber or terrorist. If men lead souls away from Christ, with their words or man-inspired, so-called holy books, the person or persons who follow are as good as dead already. They've succeeded in leading many souls to an eternity in torment without God. The world was created by God's Words. Man is destroying it with his!

Any practicing Mormon, Jehovah's Witness, follower of Muhammad and *The Koran,* Buddhist or any of these folk, once dead, will live out eternity in unfathomable torment, without second chances, none!

God cannot lie! Hell is as real as the book you're reading. Anyone, rich or poor, all ethnicities, without Christ will go to hell. Of this fact, I am one hundred percent certain.

While I'm on the subject of souls being lost, I would like to draw a simple comparison to some issues, which took place in April of 2004 in Iraq. Approximately forty people from thirteen different countries were taken hostage by Islamic militants. This, of course, struck deeply at the heart of all those who watched, especially because the kidnappings were accompanied by threats of mutilation and being burned alive. This evil caused panic, especially among the families of the hostages.

My biggest concern is that the devil and his workers are taking hostages worldwide by the millions and these hostages face a far worse ending. Yet where is the concern for these? I tell you the truth–God our Father is more than concerned. My Spirit cries within me daily, as does Christ's, for the seemingly abandoned souls, the hostages of false teachings!

Our thinking in the world today is so clouded by unspiritual, ungodly, non-Christlike answers and responses to the problems America faces today. It's no wonder that the vast majority is so afraid of total, uncontrollable destruction. I'd be scared too, scared to death. Living life without Christ is a scary way to live. *"It's a terrifying thing to fall into the hands of the living God!"* (Without Christ) (41)

Terrorists blew up a train in Madrid, Spain not that long ago and killed approximately 200 people. The devastation was obvious and so was the fear factor instilled into one of our allies. How many people on that train were ready to meet their maker? God only knows. I do know one thing for certain, though. Those on that train who didn't confess with their mouths that Jesus Christ was Lord are on their way to hell. The facts are the facts, people. A clouded decision based on false hope and false prophets come with an eternal cost!

Our world is full of clouded answers in a godless effort to solve the world's problems. I want to share with the reader a recent response to tragedy, which I feel is the epitome of our world's Spiritual blindness and ignorance. I would liken this response to doing something like trying to hold back the Hoover Dam with Popsicle sticks.

I heard on the news after the Madrid bombing that some organization immediately sent to Madrid approximately 500 psychologists to counsel the survivors and the families of the deceased. This Spiritually blind ignorance, whether done from good motives or not, still vexes my Spirit. I see the unsaved world struggling to keep hope in the hearts of people by vain, earthly methods. *"What does it profit a man to gain the whole world and forfeit his soul?"* (42)

What profit is there in calming down those who have lost a loved one and making them feel better temporarily? These people, after a time, are no better off than before. They are actually worse off. If Christ wasn't offered as a hope, the hope for a better future, the 500 psychologists might just as well have stayed home and learned more earthly psychology because they were only doing more damage by infiltrating the minds of broken people with advice that was Spiritually worthless. Five true men or women of God would have been of far more value than five million Godless psychologists. *"It is the Spirit who gives life; the flesh profits nothing!"* (43) For those who did share Christ, thank you! For those who showed the compassion of Christ, thank you!

Matthew 5, 6, and 7, referred to as "The Sermon on the Mount," is said to contain every psychological theory that man has ever conceived. With this, I totally agree. I'm qualified to make this statement as I was forced to listen to worldly psychologists by order of courts and other entities from the age of twelve until I was forty-two years old. I never got a single word of wisdom from any of them except one – he was a Christian.

"Thanks, but no thanks. I'm sorry, Dr. whoever-you-are. If your words are void of the Spirit, "the flesh profits nothing." You are wasting your time if your practice is without Biblical and Divine influence. Save your breath, please! You may write more prescriptions, but medicine won't save a soul!

Saving one soul, only one, is far more valuable to Christ than ten thousand souls temporarily comforted and given false hopes of a bright future. It's this simple. Without the Light of the world in one's life, Christ and Him alone, a person remains in darkness until the day he meets the Great Judge and Lawgiver. If a person has everything this world has to offer, and yet is without Christ, that person has nothing. If a person has nothing but Christ, that person has **everything!**

On March 21, 2004, the Palestinian founder of Hamas, Sheik Yassin, was assassinated by Israel. The Palestinians have vowed revenge, not only on Israel but on the United States. If the reader thinks this just happened by coincidence, the reader is wrong. God is tightening the thumbscrews on America. We are slowly being surrounded by His upcoming judgement. Our nation has had ample opportunity to propagate the Gospel and keep our nation safe from God's judgement by founding itself on Biblical principles.

Such a nation, founded on Biblical principals, is a theocracy, and that is what America use to be. *Theos* means "god." *Ocracy* means "government." God-government, God-centered government. Sound familiar? Of course not. If you ask a thousand children in the twelfth grade the meaning of *theocracy*, very few would know its meaning. Many Christians don't know the meaning of *theocracy*. Ask them who Monica Lewinsky is and almost everyone will know. Has anyone been to a pro football game lately? Eighty to one hundred thousand people going crazy! Cheering and screaming! When have you ever seen that many people getting that excited about Christ? When's the last time you saw someone build a billion dollar church? Billion dollar football stadiums are all over the United States! How many preachers get paid 40 million every 5 years? Our priorities are a little mixed up, don't you think? Do you think Jesus is watching or worshipping sports? No! He's worshipping the throne and watching lost souls!

This is sad, very sad. As with the death of Yassin, God is using many different peoples as enemies to bring about the demise of the "proud" United States of America in order to urge its people to repentance. I hope this book urges repentance. Otherwise, I have wasted a lot of my time and my family's. I've made this sacrifice for only one reason–to instill into the hearts of all who read or hear the pages of this book the vital, urgent, desperate need for repentance in the United States of America and the need for repentance in the lost souls we encounter in our daily lives.

I am like a horse with blinders, a horse with a single focused mission. *"I have set my face like a flint"* (44) for Christ, His cries, His call and His mission. It is only by the grace and love of God and his Christ that I'm even alive to write these words. Many times I came within inches or seconds of being an obituary. God has spared me countless times for one reason and you're reading it. You are reading the words of a man who lived like the scum of the earth and slept under bridges in forty-below-zero weather. I have accepted my call, surrendered (after much chastisement – "power is perfected in weakness"), and was filled with the Holy Ghost. *"God is no respecter of persons."* (45) He will do the same for anyone who asks.

The Scriptures are crystal clear. Eventually, this world is coming to an end. Just as Christ condemned the religious system of His day, so the Spirit condemns the same in our day. (Matthew 23) Since the year 2000, new religions have increased at an alarming rate. Jesus said, *"See to it that no one misleads you.* (46) I guess that has been ignored. Several thousand souls each year are drawn into cults like Mormonism and Jehovah's Witnesses. The reason I seem to isolate these two is that they are the biggest threat to Christianity and our mission. God has been consistent in warning us but to no avail. Today, an estimated twenty million Americans are in cults. Religious deception is running rampant in our midst. We, as Christians, are temples of the Holy Spirit, yet the Lord's words ring true regarding the spiritual condition of "religious" people today. *"Behold, your house is left unto you desolate!"* (47)

The weakness and shallowness of worldly worship and religion that's been tainted by the flesh, which profits nothing, are about to be brought to trial and found wanting. Ritual and ceremonial Christians; health, wealth and prosperity Christians; self-esteem psychology Christians; non-Bible-reading Christians; and self-serving Christians, beware! Heed the words of one dynamic in power: *"I know your deeds, that you are neither cold nor hot;* **I would that you were cold or hot. So because you are lukewarm,** *and neither hot nor cold, I will spit you out of My mouth. Because you say, I am wealthy and have need of nothing,"* (Does this shoe fit America or what!) *and you do not know that you are wretched and miserable and poor and blind and naked, I advise you to buy from Me gold refined by fire, that you may become rich,* (best advice a man could ever get right there) *and white garments, that you may clothe yourself and that the shame* (I think America has forgotten the meaning of this word) *of your nakedness* (the real you) *may not be revealed; and eye salve to anoint your eyes, that you may see!"* (48)

I can just picture some cultic, Spiritless entrepreneur cornering the market on eye salve prior to Christ's return. Why not? The founder of Jehovah's Witnesses was selling "Miraculous Wheat Seed," said to produce far more than any other seed. Actually, it turned out to be of lesser quality than that available in his day (49)

Deception surrounds America today and most accept it as normal. The trash on TV is accepted as normal. I was happy to see so many souls take such a great interest in the blockbuster, *The Passion of the Christ,* by Mel Gibson, but I also saw in the Spirit some interesting issues. Let me share the thoughts I had.

Why was the movie such a box office success, one of the greatest of all time? Because it was the best movie ever made about Jesus? Not necessarily. Was it the most Biblically accurate. Not necessarily. Was it the cool effects? No. What was it then? It was nothing less to a man or a woman with Spiritual eyes than a wake-up call from God, a warning alerting God's people to take notice of how desperately hungry this entire nation is for Christ, for truth, for peace, for comfort and most of all, security. Obviously, Jesus Christ is all these qualities and gives all these qualities, and, may I add, for free! You don't have to wait in line or try to find a parking spot.

Christians need to wake up and take in the harvest right now. If we don't harvest this crop of souls, guess who is going to? Here are some of the answers to this question: New Age movements, transcendental meditation, alcohol, drugs, prisons, pornographers, nightclubs, phone sex, video games, MTV, psychics, gay men, lesbians, Mormons, Jehovah's Witnesses, Muslims, Buddhists, Kabalah, positive thinking seminars, Paxil, Vicodin, Oxycontin, Synthetic Drugs, Heroin, Zoloft, Lithium, Thorazine, Zanex, suicide, crime, and corporate, hedonistic America. *"I would like that none would perish, but all would come to repentance to eternal life!"*(50) It certainly didn't take America long to make the transition from "Leave It to Beaver" to "Jerry Springer," from "Golly gee, Dad" to bleep-bleep trash talk. It sickens me to watch things like Madonna french-kissing Brittany Spears (every teenager's idol) on TV. And the thing I fear the most is that those who watch this evil *"Don't even know how to blush!"* (51) Just look at who 'Hanna Montana' turned out to be! Or should I say what she turned out to be!

The Lord speaks clearly of giving certain sinners *"over to a depraved mind."* (52) Doesn't that word, *depraved*, just fit perfectly in describing America's morality? It fits like a glove. Everything in our culture is slowly being twisted, even terminologies. People in certain nightclub scenes, for example, will ask a person, "Are you gay or straight?" Now, what's that supposed to mean? Certainly, a depraved sinner, deep in the mire of his or her own shameful lifestyle couldn't use words like Godly, or *normal* or *heterosexual*. Instead, the crooked themselves call it straight.

This whole gay marriage thing and ordaining gay men and lesbian women to ecclesiastical office is to me incomprehensible. When I saw an admitted gay man on national television become a bishop, my Spiritual ears heard the fires of hell being kindled. Just like a large gas grill that's been overloaded with gas fumes igniting. Did you hear it? Yes, YOU! Because if you didn't, drop this book, find a Bible and start devouring every word in it, lest you help kindle the flames. *"He who has ears to hear, let him hear,"* (53) lest he perish. All I can say is I'm tremendously impressed with God's patience. This entire issue is absolutely demonic, depraved iniquity and gross immorality. Homosexual behavior is the epitome of Satan's nature in distorting the Holy image of our Christ. Just guess who I put most of the blame on? Christians, self-serving Christians, who will not sacrifice getting out of their comfort zone and fighting spiritually the good fight of faith. How did the gay marriage issues and homosexuality issue become so easily accepted when Christians far outweigh their numbers in society? Because the majority of Christians just kept silent when these laws of gay marriage were being PASSED! What happened to our zeal Christians? The scripture says truly, "because lawlessness has increased, most peoples love has grown cold."

Did you know that Christianity and its teachings used to counsel both homosexuals and lesbians – has the highest success rate in the U.S. in restoring them back to a natural, heterosexual lifestyle? God's word once again brings the darkness into light.

There is zero evidence supporting gay activist theories that their behavior is genetic either. A dysfunctional relationship in the family between parents and children is the number one 'cause found' through unbiased research. There are other factors, but this is the most understood and agreed upon by researchers. If it was genetic, how do you explain identical twins (one gay and one not!) It simply disproves the propaganda used by homosexuals and lesbians to continue their lustful, ungodly desires.

In my opinion (I've studied scripture since I was thirteen and am now fifty-two), the best book I've ever read on the subject was 'The Church & Homosexuality' by Merton P. Strommen, 2nd Edition. He includes both sides of the story and undeniable facts. This fine Christian man makes it crystal clear with research quotes from many other researchers and psychiatrist's and psychologists, the reasons for this behavior and what the Church should do about it in a loving, non-judgmental way.

Another Theologian Strommen quotes is Robert Gagnon's book published in 2001, 'The Bible & Homosexual Practice'. In it, he says "The Bible unequivocally defines same-sex intercourse as a sin." Also "Same-sex intercourse constitutes an inexcusable rebellion against the intentional design of the created order."

Leviticus 18:22 & 20:13; I Corinthians 6:9-11; 1 Timothy 1:10-11; Romans 1:26-27 and 1:18-23 makes clear God's position that homosexuality and lesbianism are unnatural and of no origin but sin. The only way anyone, religious, gay, worldly or otherwise can interpret this in any other way, knows nothing of Hermeneutics. Hermeneutics is the science of interpretation of an author's work, particularly related to the interpretation of Scripture. In this science, it is recognized that there are two types of interpretation - Eisegesis (Ice-A-Gee-Sis) and Exegesis (X-Ah-Gee-Sis). A true student of Hermeneutics is referred to as an 'exegete', taking out of a written text (the Bible), only that which was intended by the writer, taking into consideration things like culture, history, context, original language and so on. Also, which in the case of Scripture, the character of God, His consistency, holiness, hatred and judgement of sin done with impunity, and forgiveness through His son, Jesus Christ.

An Eisegēte is a person (usually done by an individual or group of individuals) like gay activist groups for example, that do an improper method of interpreting Scripture and introducing their own ideas into a text. The prefix of the Greek word, the 'eis' means "into", "a bringing in". The second part of the word means "to lead or to guide". All eisegētes have either a lack of knowledge or have ulterior motives. The latter is the case with those who twist Scripture to achieve their goals. For example, justifying the election of gay and lesbian bishops and pastors in the church today. Obviously, most Christians today have no idea of the future implications of these decisions on the minds and hearts of our vulnerable children. If they did, this never would have happened. We stood by and let it happen. What now?

The great reformer Martin Luther wrote in regards to a proper interpretation of Scripture, "No violence (no changing or distorting) is to be done to the words of God, whether by man or angel; but the Scriptures are to be retained in their simplest meaning where ever possible and to be understood in their grammatical and literal sense unless the context plainly forbids." He also wrote, "the Holy Spirit is the plainest writer and speaker in Heaven and on Earth, therefore, His words cannot have more than one, and the very simplest sense."

There is much more to be said about gay and lesbians getting ordained in the Church, while still practicing homosexuality and lesbianism and how we as Christians let it get to this possibly, irreversible point. I hope this is a wake-up call to all Christians reading or hearing this message.

I want to make clear here also, we are all required to hate the sin and love the sinner! Our job is to reach out and do our best to bring these individuals to Christ. The Scripture tells us "all have sinned and fall short of the Glory of God, there is none righteous, no not even one!" Keep in mind this also; we have already allowed the work of the activists to infiltrate our schools and Holy ground, the Church. How long will it be before we allow them to rewrite the Word of God? We can love everyone, but we are responsible for what we allow to destroy our hearts, mind and spirits and those of our children's. "He who has ears to hear, let him hear!"

Spiritual sloth is running rampant among Christians today. The Word of God has not only been neglected in the church and at home but even those who know God's Word falter when it comes to offering it to those obviously in need. Most have kept it to save only themselves and the America we live in today clearly shows the results we've reaped. No planting, no fruits to gather! The grim reaper will gather these, though, with a thank-you to God's diluted body, a body that's not much different in outward expressions of love on the whole than the people without salvation. It's just like Americans in the twenty-first century to take advantage of a good thing while it lasts, in this case, God's grace.

Nothing grieves my Spirit more than the years I took advantage of God's grace. I'm ashamed of all the souls I let slip through my fingers while seeking my own desires. Because of all or our selfishness (including my own) with our great gift of salvation, the world is once again filled with violence and corruption: corrupt credit default swaps which destroyed the housing market, gang filled cities, drug cartels, murder in every city in America. Did you know that over 165,000 men, women and children have been murdered on the US/Mexico border over drugs?! Many of these souls have already been 'given over to their own desires' until the judgement.

It's not coincidental that as my pen wrote down the words, "violence and corruption," that my Spirit was immediately drawn to the book of Genesis, chapter 6. I think it important here to interject how my Spirit, as I write, always seems to draw me to relevant Scriptures. The reason I'm explaining this to you is that today, as I was reading my work to a Christian man for insight about my writing, he commented with a question. "Alan, how is it that you're able to write all these things page after page and come up with all this?" I answered simply, *"I can do all things through Christ who strengthens me."* (54) I have the Word of God written on my heart.

Again, not by coincidence, after writing those two words, "violence and corruption," God led me to Genesis, where the exact same two words are used to describe the characteristics of human behavior which demanded God's intervention, leading to a destruction, namely, the Great Flood. Please read the following scripture and see if the same shoe fits America today:

"Now the earth was corrupt in the sight of God and the earth was filled with violence. God looked upon the earth (Guess what. He's still looking.) and behold, it was corrupt; for all the flesh had corrupted their

way upon the earth. Then God said to Noah, 'The end of all flesh has come before Me; for the earth is filled with violence because of them; and behold, I am about to destroy them with the earth!'" (55)

All I can say to that is WOW! This is serious business. Take note that God didn't just destroy the people. He also destroyed the earth, all of it. Why? Because our God is a thorough God. He hates sin and defilement. When God purposes complete destruction, He misses nothing.

The fact that God destroyed the earth along with the people should be a good indicator of the depth of our God's Holiness. He saw man's defilement was so severe that even his creation, earth, was tainted and defiled by man. This is what you'd call a Holy Righteous housecleaning.

In retrospect, I'm reminded that we've yet to hear a peep from anyone living in Sodom or Gomorrah. Not only that, from what I've read, no one has yet been able to one hundred percent identify the remains of the city, which Almighty God destroyed. The people who do claim to have found the site of Sodom and Gomorrah say that the site contains a vast amount of sulfur deposits. Sounds like a great place to start a match factory. There is just one problem, though—no survivors, not even one!

I can see why homosexuals and lesbians avoid the Bible. It's impossible to *"rightly divide the Word of Truth"* (56) and justify an obvious abomination. Even with our Lord's judgement of AIDS, these individuals still go around walking on the hot coals of judgement beneath their feet. (See Romans 1) Because of American Christians' indifference and tolerance to this abomination, it is seen at the levels to which it has grown. Obviously, when openly gay women become hosts of their own TV shows in America and their ratings are high, Christian voices have clearly missed their mark in Biblically refuting, reproving, and condemning this evil.

Gay and lesbian individuals are deceived in their hearts. When I see these types now raising children, the vexation that arises in my Spirit does not have a word anywhere in the English language to describe my torment.

I truly cannot fathom the righteous indignation seething in the heavens. The fact that no alarm has sounded deep in the hearts of

Christian America disturbs me deeply. America needs to *"put on the full armor of God"* (57) and take up *"the sword of the Spirit"* (58) while there is still time. I am not an eschatologist, nor do I rack my brain trying to figure out the day when Christ is returning. *"Behold, now is the day of salvation,"* (59) saith the Lord.

I already know in my spirit, confirmed by the words of Scripture and clear signs of the times, that the clock is running out. If people claiming to be Christians, in a time such as this, do not sense the impending doom, then I will unequivocally tell them that there's something wrong with their relationship to the Word of God. I'm not just sure about this statement. I'm positive! Even lost and blind Muslims have enough sense to outright condemn homosexuality, gay marriage and civil unions.

By the way, whoever designated the term, "civil union" to describe two gay sinners living together ought to have their head examined. What on earth is "civil" about any of this unrestrained licentiousness? The term, "Civil union" only hides the devil's intent.

The "violence and corruption" described in Genesis 6 is clearly characteristic of today's world. So the question remains, what is God going to do and when is He going to do it. I am going to briefly give the reader the best explanation my Spirit can now give while staying within the mandates and guidelines of Scripture.

The first question of what God is going to do is elementary. He's going to do exactly the same as He has always done in the past when His creation gets out of control. He's going to destroy all unrepentant, Godless, sinners not washed by the blood of Christ.

The second question of how soon is slightly more complex. The Gospel of Matthew, chapter 24, which I personally feel gives the most definitive information on the subject on when the Lord will return, immediately narrows down the scope of our investigation on this much inquired issue. Let me begin with 24:36: *"But of the day and hour no one knows not even the angels of heaven, nor the Son, but the Father alone."* (61) This statement limits one's research to following the "signs" in order to have one's best idea of when the Lord's coming is close at our door. So, if then we don't know the day or the hour, what do we know?"

Well, a lot actually. The Bible is explicitly clear to a person with Spiritual eyes about the signs to watch for the time of the return of Christ. The second thing I know for certain is one sign, which seems to be way overlooked by Christians today. It is also one of the surest ways to sense within the inner man, in our Spirit, that the Lord is near. I'm referring to the character of God, which never, ever, ever changes. NEVER! *"Jesus Christ is the same yesterday and today, yes and forever!"* (62) He's also perfect in His constancy in judging sin. Of this, there is no doubt.

Understanding God's character, not on the surface, but a deep understanding derived from a consistent and profound relationship with God's Word is the key ingredient missing in Christianity today. It is also the key ingredient for any Spiritual man or woman in their ability to discern deep truths and, more importantly, revelations of God's Word which prompt urgency for lost souls and the dangers, which lie ahead for an unspiritual nation.

Christians are still a minority and this saddens the heart of our Savior. The Scripture tells us that *"he who is Spiritual appraises all things."* (63) Doing a Spiritual appraisal of any given situation, Spiritual or earthly, and being accurate is clearly a gift. Nothing less than the work of the Holy Spirit of God the Father and the Lord Jesus Christ can accomplish this. To God be the glory!

This entire book is a true Spiritual appraisal. Am I now boasting? No! I understand God, that's all. I've been studying *"to show myself approved unto God."* (64) I'm doing nothing less than *"handling accurately or rightly dividing the word of truth."* (65) I've been doing this since I was fourteen years old during good times and bad. If I were to boast, it would only be that I know and understand God deeply.

"Thus says the Lord, 'Let not a wise man boast of his wisdom, and let not the mighty man boast of his might, let not a rich man boast of his riches; but let him who boasts boast of this, THAT HE UNDERSTANDS AND KNOWS ME, that I am THE LORD who exercises lovingkindness, JUSTICE, and righteousness on earth; for I delight in these things,'" (66)

We must be careful in verbalizing a spiritual appraisal and be sure we speak for God. I cringe when people use the terminology,

"God told me thus...thus... and thus..." God's Holy Word confirms my appraisals are accurate. What more does one need?

We must never forget our God is omniscient, all knowing, past and present and future. God didn't tell Isaiah the exact date Christ would be born, but He did tell him, and us, approximately 700 years beforehand that Christ would be born of a virgin. Now, because God can't lie, it happened just as He said.

There are numerous prophecies in Scripture, which have been fulfilled to the letter. Isaiah and Jeremiah are full of these. Of course, the most exciting of all prophecies are the ones, which predict Christ's second coming. I believe, based on the consistent character of God throughout all of recorded Biblical history covering a period of approximately 6,500 years in the narrative of Holy Scripture, and also based on His consistent character in dealing with sinful nations and peoples, that Christ's second coming will be in this century. I say this without the slightest hesitation and without conflict from God's Holy Spirit. Inner peace, the *"peace of God which surpasses all comprehension,"* (67) is my guide now and will continue to be.

It should be obvious that I'm not picking any specific dates. Even attempting to do this is not only a complete waste of time but it is clearly self-induced Spiritual Biblical ignorance. The old Millerite movement of the early nineteenth century found this out with an embarrassing show of cult-like ignorance.

What I'm saying specifically is that I feel that exact same sense of impending doom that Isaiah felt before Assyria struck Israel, the Northern Kingdom. I feel the same fear and sadness Jeremiah expressed before Babylon finished off Judah, the Southern Kingdom. It's very important to keenly evaluate God's character throughout the period of the two invasions by "foreigners" on God's beloved nations and peoples and specifically what took place, who stood by and watched and, most important of all, why God allowed the destruction.

Why did God allow Judah to watch Israel being attacked and taken captive? The answer is simple. For exactly the same reason God is allowing other nations today to watch our nation being attacked by "foreigners." It is a clear warning to all the world and those watching of God's imminent judgement for an "iniquity" which is almost complete.

Let me explain. In Genesis, as God is speaking to Abraham, He is foretelling Abraham about a specific timeline in which God himself is going to follow. In the timeline, God reveals to Abraham the reason for the temporary delay of the children of Israel taking full possession of the Promised Land in Palestine. God says, *"Then in the fourth generation, they* (the Israelites in slavery in Egypt) *shall return here* (to the Promised Land) *"FOR THE INIQUITY OF THE AMORITES IS NOT YET COMPLETE."* (68) The Amorites were all the idolatrous Canaanite tribes in Palestine.

Many important things come into focus here for the eyes of a Spiritual man or woman. The most important of these things are the characteristics of a Holy God, who, from His Words, makes clear that there is a limit to the amount of iniquity (self-willed lawlessness) that God will allow before judgement must be handed down. The cup of God's wrath does eventually get full, as depicted here, as in Noah's time which brought a flood of destruction, as in the time of Sodom and Gomorrah, as in the time of Jonah, when Ninevah's iniquity was complete and God was about to release His wrath. Only Jonah's preaching the hard Truth brought about the required repentance, which saved that entire city. The same picture is seen in Isaiah's, Jeremiah's, Ezekiel's and Daniel's time when both Israel and Judah received a crushing blow from the hand of our righteous Judge and Lawgiver. The same God and His same character have followed mankind's every thought and action right up to September 11th in New York City when God warned America and those watching of His nearness and their need for repentance. Does America think it is exempt from Divine Judgment? Think again! I want to remind the reader once again, God didn't do it, however, He allowed it!

The Scripture says, "God is no respecter of persons!" (69) There is no need for me to try to list the sins, which brought this judgement of God to America. Time and materials might not accommodate such a venture.

It appears to me, as I gaze into the heart of God that the wrath of the cup of God's anger has begun to be poured out upon America in such a way that we have no defense. I believe this wrath will soon pour out upon America in Biblical proportions.

When a student of God's Word (a Spiritual student–there is a huge difference) meditates on His consistent character all throughout the Holy Word of God, it would be almost impossible to draw any other conclusion than the one I've put before you. And that conclusion is THE TIME IS AT HAND!

I'm not going to waste any time discussing pre-tribulation, mid-tribulation or post-tribulation theories. It doesn't really matter who is right. All will require the same thing. A man or woman of God must be fully prepared to speak the truth written on their hearts, and to defend their beliefs to the point of death, period.

The prophecies in Scripture, such as Matthew 24, which to me personally, is the one which speaks the clearest in reference to Christ's return and the situations which will arise and take place just prior to His return. These seem to be of vital importance to the Christian. I must say, though, that unequivocally I've found that just simply following and observing God's character in His past dealings with other nations speaks volumes more than any isolated passage of Scripture. When God's unchanging, predictable character (predictable to the man of the Spirit) is combined with His written warnings in Scripture, I think it's high time to get very, very serious and sincere in our Christian walks and fulfill the much neglected "Great Commission" and the rest of the mandates in Holy Scripture. Even the Lost who are Spiritually blind can see and sense the hand of something very powerful taking place in America today. Why did God allow our government to get caught tapping all the telephones and cell phones of our allies in October 2013? Because God is slowly removing our protection! Our friends! Our false pride and protection!

The reason, which I stated before, for the crowded theaters when Mel Gibson's movie, *The Passion of the Christ,* played on the big screen is fear. People are scared, very scared, and for good reason. A person who hasn't received Christ still has a tremendous fear of being without God for eternity, even though he or she is not aware that this is exactly what is taking place in their souls created by God and for God. The soul automatically and, better yet, naturally yearns for its creator anytime something threatens its existence. Why do so many people on their deathbeds waste no more time in trying to contact their creator? It is only natural. God gave us life. Whom do children run to when they are afraid? They run to the closest thing to God they know, Mom or Dad.

When a twenty-first-century soul senses impending doom, it cannot but seek Spiritual guidance. It is a natural response to God's beloved creation. Since most in America today have neither Spiritual parents nor associates, they inevitably turn to the media, the babysitter of America. Am I wrong on this? Has not our society used the media to drown out the constant beckoning of its creator? Of course, it has! So what better place to go during such a time as this than to the movies. Does the reader think the timing of Mel Gibson's movie is a coincidence? I think not! Don't be foolish, people, God is knocking at the door of His lost sheep's heart, before the real final finale.

What will Christians do—watch as lost souls are taken eternally captive by the real enemy, Satan. It's neither Al Qaeda nor the Muslim extremists. These are just instruments of Satan, which God is allowing for His Divine and Holy purposes of Judgement. The growth of false and cult-like religions is simply due to the negligence of those who have been entrusted with the duty of mightily and fearlessly bringing forth God's word in totality, especially within the home. If you don't do it someone else will. His name is Satan! Again, character comes into play. Only this time it's ours, not God's.

We, too, are predictable creatures, aren't we? When God told His children to enter the promised land, they were given absolutely clear instructions to *"drive out all the inhabitants of the land"* (70) from before them (so as not to be corrupted by the Canaanites' ungodly practices (such as what we have complacently allowed in America today) and destroy all their molten images and demolish all their high places. Did you notice how many times that God used the word *all*? God wants NO evil influences to corrupt His people or His plan for redemption. Israel, just as we, failed to completely eradicate sinful influence. Israel's failure resulted, as we know, in the Assyrian and Babylonian captivities. Our failure has resulted in the violent and corrupt, ungodly societies in which we are held captive today. Our children's hearts and minds are open game mom and dad!

What's more important? Paying for that 5,000 square foot house or letting your children pay with their souls!

The Bible says, *"His own iniquities* (lawlessness void of God's laws) *will capture the wicked, and he* (America) *will be held with the cords of his sin. HE WILL DIE FOR LACK OF INSTRUCTION, and in the greatness of his folly, he will go astray! For the ways of a man* (America) *are before the Lord and he watches ALL His paths!"* (71)

I think if we, as Christians, were to expose to the Godless today, the truth in the Scripture I just quoted about God watching everything, they would probably run to the mountains and hills in fear of Almighty God. The Godless around us, though, have little fear if any because we have not instilled this in them by our Holy living or the fearless proclamation of God's love and judgement. We allowed idolatry to run rampant in our midst. And don't forget, in God's midst too, for Christ lives within us to those who love Him. *"Christ in you—the Eternal Hope of glory"* (72)

The First Commandment and its repeated violations have caused more loss and devastation to God's former people than any other sin. This is identical to America today. We have the same disrespect for God's Holy and righteous jealousy as they had 3,400 years ago when Joshua began conquering the Promised Land. People forget so easily that which is important to our God. *"For, I the Lord your God, am a jealous God!"* (73)

God has not in the past, nor will He now allow the sin, which He hates so much–IDOLATRY! The number of idols in America today far outweighs its number of cities. Here again, time and materials certainly would not allow me to list America's sins of idolatry because they are voluminous. In my estimation, the number is beyond calculations. We are now at the recompense stage.

Here we see the characteristics of man's nature, the continual propensity toward sin. Job very eloquently describes these phenomena when he says, "For affliction does not come from the dust, neither does trouble sprout from the ground, for man is born for trouble, just as sparks fly upward." (74) I think contemplation of this single verse alone is a great reason to want a Savior.

My point in all this is that it would serve Christians well who truly want to know and do God's will, to begin to analyze the consistent character traits of God and man, and upon this investigation, hopefully, draw a conclusion. If this conclusion is based on history, it will show where we are headed as a nation. The results of such a conclusion should be immediate responsive action to avert the spilling of the wrath of the cup of God's anger. I see this cup in God's hand and He is slowly tipping the cup to spill out its contents on a foolish, Spiritually lazy, idolatrous, hedonistic, selfish, and Godless nation!

This nation has for 225 years been given the uncontested freedom of religion and the practice thereof. This, itself, is the reason our judgement in America is and will continue to be so severe. We were a favored and blessed nation, appointed by God Himself, and we did exactly the same thing with this privilege as the children of Israel did when God gave them settlement in the Promised Land, fertile and awesome in all respects. Look what we've done to the world's ecology! Thousand-year-old glaciers are one hundred percent gone! They have disappeared from the face of the Earth! Hello? Anybody home?

Man today is so ignorant of his futility without Christ and also the vanity which surrounds his existence. A fervent study of Ecclesiastes is invaluable to the Christian worker, (as is all Scripture) for a revelation in understanding the pointlessness of a life lived without Christ and for God's purposes. The last verses of chapter twelve nicely summarize the entire book and its purpose in the message Solomon wants to convey. I won't quote it because I hope everyone will read it.

Too many books today try to give us crumbs off the Bread of Life. It seems pointless when no man can live properly without all of God's Word. We must *"receive the Word implanted which is able to save your soul!"* (75) We are becoming a defeated force in this world today Christians because God's work is done *"not by might, nor by power, but by My Spirit," says* the Lord of Hosts. (76) Without God's Word and the fearlessness that accompanies it, our mission to save souls is greatly diminished.

America may be too powerful of a nation to be taken physically captive like Judah and Israel were, but "be ye not deceived," we can and are being taken captive Spiritually. This is far more dangerous because that captivity comes with eternal consequences.

I talked earlier about the importance of individual Christians beginning to contemplate God's consistent character and the benefits of this, over trying to use isolated passages of Scripture as a guide to understanding the clear picture of Spiritual reality today.

Another absolutely vital aspect of our faith, which seems almost non-existent today, even in Christian circles, is an **eternal perspective** in all of our daily lives, our relationships with our children, our associates, our teaching, our preaching, our giving, our forgiving, and the way we use God's money. The list is endless because an eternal perspective is necessary in almost every aspect of a Christian's life if he or she is to be an effective messenger for God. An effective messenger is a true workman.

People are so desperate just to maintain their daily comforts they've grown so accustomed to, that eternity is the last thing on their minds. Living one day at a time might be Alcoholics Anonymous' way to victory and that way of life may, in fact, keep a man sober for many, many years. Yet, if this man stays sober for ninety-nine years, what profit does this man gain if after all that effort he loses his soul? Anyone, Christian or not, living life without the eternal perspective each and every day in their hearts and on their minds is merely *"striving after the wind!"* (77)

God's Word alone and no other book, considered holy or otherwise, can bring us to a consistency in keeping an eternal perspective at the forefront of our hearts and minds. Fleshly food feeds the flesh. Spiritual food feeds the Spirit. Every single thing God ever said or did came from an eternal perspective. A Holy focus is an eternal focus. A true Christian life is lived in eternity, by faith, NOW!

God instills eternity in the heart of all human creation. Solomon said, *"He has made everything appropriate in its time. He has also set eternity in their heart."* (78) When an individual, through his or her relationship with God's Word, receives the gift of eternal perspective, he or she needs no prodding or goading for motivation in sharing Christ. A person who has the "mind of Christ" or eternal perspective is inwardly compelled by the dynamic power of the Holy Ghost, almost seemingly without effort. It just comes so naturally and fearlessly. It is God's gift and grace combined. I pray that those reading this book should have kindled within themselves the fires and motivation of an eternal perspective.

I cannot overemphasize the importance people, of the tremendous benefits of receiving the eternal perspective in unison with God and His Holy Spirit. From Genesis to the end of Revelation, we walk the road of God's eternal perspective. It is important to remember, though, that prior to anyone receiving gifts of revelation from God, a man or woman must first be brought to a place in their heart of contrition to even begin the transformation of their souls from fleshly to Spiritual mindedness.

The scripture is clear why the flesh must be controlled by the Spirit to make Spiritual growth a reality. Paul, in his letter to the church at Corinth, was struggling with many issues, one of which was the Corinthians' misunderstanding of the Holy Spirit's ministry, in revealing Spiritual truths to people of the world void of God's spirit. Paul says, *"But a natural man does not accept the things of the Spirit of God; for they are foolishness to him, and he cannot understand them, because they are Spiritually appraised."* (79)

That verse is so clear and concise! A *'natural'* man with a **natural** mind is **doomed!**

An individual must be humbled before he can be of any use to God. As John the Baptist rightly spoke, *"He* (Jesus) *must increase, but I must decrease."* (80) King Solomon taught repeatedly that "Before honor comes humility!" (81) Being saved from sin and death is truly a great honor. Humility coming before honor is a truth I personally can attest to.

The Lord has been righteously diligent in keeping me humble for fifty-two years now, and I hope he never stops. *"It is good For me that I was afflicted* (eight years behind bars) *that I may learn Thy statutes!"* (82) *"Before I was afflicted, I went astray, but now I keep Thy Word."* (83)

I'm dangerous, very dangerous without Christ. I've always been my own worst enemy. Without Christ, all people fall into this category. It took thirty years of God's faithful discipline to bring about my true and final surrender. I thank God for His patience and undeserved favor (grace) and one part of His Holy Word, one single verse that I held on to like precious treasure. It was mine, against all human odds and countless people verbalizing my guaranteed failure in life. I held it against every evil spirit's lie of my hopelessness and utterly impossible transformation. I needed it against forces that only I can speak of their intensity, with their evil motives and desire to kill me, not only physically but mentally also.

I went through thirty years of torment, from which only a mighty and powerful God could deliver me. This God's name is Jesus Christ. This is the God I chose of all the thousands of gods the world offers today. It was only this God that truly delivers and keeps His promises. I knew, by faith, that He kept His promise of bringing us a Savior, so I also knew by faith that the words I kept precious to my heart and mind would someday be fulfilled for me as long as I continued to believe them. The words I used to win every attempt by the devil to kill me or make me commit suicide were *"I am confident of the very thing, that He* (Jesus Christ) *who began a good work in you will be faithful to complete it, until the day of Christ Jesus!"* (84)

From the first day I picked up and read the entire Bible in a state institution at around the age of fourteen, I was filled with the hopeless feelings everyone around me felt and then, *"I found His words and I ate them and they became for me a joy and the delight of my heart." (85) Still* today I hold tightly on to that special promise knowing the dangers and temptation our society is filled with. I've finally accepted that I'm His child and He will have it no other way as long as I believe in His Son. The peace, which has filled my life now after I've surrendered to God's purposes, is quite indescribable in worldly, spiritless terms. This world with all its pomp and pride has nothing available to offer which brings this type of peace. Take it from me. I'm a fifty-two-year old veteran of the greatest Spiritual warfare one can endure without death or suicide halting the battle - verbal abuse, physical abuse, sexual abuse (not from my family), emotional abuse, drug and alcohol abuse.

King David's words recorded in Psalm 131 seem to perfectly describe my feelings of peace and new attitude: *"O Lord, my heart is not proud, nor my eyes haughty; nor do I involve myself in great matters,* (This statement alone is a miracle of grace) *or in things too difficult for me. Surely I have composed and quieted my soul; like a weaned child rests against his mother, my soul is like a weaned child within me."* (86) This statement clearly depicts a man who has stopped wrestling with God, trying to live for himself, and showing religious pretense at the same time.

It's truly amazing how, after my surrender to God, that certain passages come to life in a way they never did before. God continually confirms His Word as he has since the beginning of creation. It's just so awesome to feel that I'm part of God's plan. I was truly a nobody and now I'm more than a somebody. I'm a child of the King, the greatest King that has ever existed since the beginning of time.

If you want to talk about an inheritance, folks, this is one to get excited about. This inheritance is permanent and better yet, eternal. I pray to God that millions more will become living examples of Psalm 131, like Christ, the Word incarnate.

God gives us inner peace so we can focus on His mission of saving souls. If our minds are constantly hindered and fully absorbed with worldly concerns, where does that leave Christ's commission? Exactly where it is today, taking third or fourth place on the priority list of a Christian's life. When souls are not our first priority in life, our priorities are simply wrong.

The very reason I wrote this book is on behalf of unsaved souls. The Holy Spirit has compelled me to do so. If I accomplish only one thing as a result of the publication of this book, I hope it would be that all readers would feel the great sense of urgency within my heart and soul to make their relationship to the Word of God the most important thing in their lives and the lives of everyone they ever meet.

Without a national revival of the exaltation of God's Holy, life-saving Word and the expression of its vitalness for each living soul on earth, we are going to lose one of the biggest, ripest, most abundant harvests of souls in the history of our nation. Christians are already a minority. That's detrimental enough to our cause. The far worse problem is that within our small minority, we have even a much smaller number of individuals who are Biblically sound and ready for the Spiritual war which pounds on the door of our once great spiritual nation.

Talk about being short on troops, Christian armies are the prophetic fulfillment of that statement. War is now here Christians, today! Don 't be ignorant of your Spiritual assessment of our present situation in America. Always remember:

"For though we walk in the flesh, we do not war according to the flesh, for the weapons of our warfare are not of the flesh, but divinely powerful for the destruction of fortresses! We are (supposed to be) *destroying every lofty thing raised up against the knowledge of God."* (87)

With all the false religions surrounding America today, it is quite evident that very few Christians from our whole number have destroyed things, which have raised themselves up against the (Bible) knowledge of God! If this issue specifically isn't addressed NOW, the chances of us, as a Christian army, having victory over our enemies, the multitudinous enemies of our Holy Gospel are getting tremendously slim.

The Word of God is sharper than any two-edged sword. I love the insight which Martin Luther had in regard to where a Christian's power lies. The words of his great song are clearly nothing less than Divine inspiration: "A mighty fortress is our God, a bulwark never failing. Our helper He is against the flood of mortal ills prevailing. (Sounds just like today, mortally ill) And still our ancient foe doth seek to work us woe, his craft and power are great, (now Satan's using terrorists right inside America) and armed with cruel hate (Osama Bin Laden) on earth is not his equal." And the song goes on; the most widely sung Christian hymn in the world today. Sadly, it is the least conceived in the hearts of God's people. My favorite line of the entire song is "ONE LITTLE WORD SHALL FELL HIM."

Here was a man who truly knew the awesome, undefeatable, indescribably powerful weapon we have against all evil, within the Word of God alone. Even ONE LITTLE WORD! Let any fool bring his case of evil intent before Almighty God and come out unscathed. God's Word is omnipotent! How else does one suppose Job was able to be so patient with God during his unfathomable calamities? I will tell you how in Job's own words: *"I have treasured the words of His mouth more than my necessary food."* (88)

What about David? Can we conceive a true picture of one-tenth of what David lived through and then reflect on his comments about God's Word and how he could never have survived without it? If we can, we begin to get a glimpse of the vitalness of what America is missing today while starving itself of God's Word.

The Spiritual starvation in America, proportionate to its population, is beyond epidemic. The consequences don't even compare to those physical in nature. Only God can save us through Christ and His atoning blood and His Word.

In Psalm 119, an amazing 173 of the 176 verses make reference to God's Word. This alone should be enough to cement in the souls of Christians that which is most important of all, Truth! God's Word is that Truth! For example, what good does a liturgy do? How many souls have tradition-practicing churches saved? How many unsaved people do we invite to our church Bible studies?

What good does it do for a preacher to stand on a pulpit and preach week after week and not address nor utterly condemn those things attacking our very existence as Christians today. Those issues slowly and subtly eating away at the foundation of our faith. These issues are destroying and taking captive the minds and hearts of our children in the media, in the classrooms and everywhere else we turn our heads. Why would one suppose all of God's great martyrs spoke so boldly and fearlessly about the truth of the infectious issues gnawing away at everything Christ died for? Isn't this the very heart of the reason why Paul wrote his letters of concern to the churches he established? He wrote because things were going awry. The issues were obviously important enough to Christians to make the letters of the Christian New Testament of our faith and canonize it.

The hearts of martyrs were moved by the Spirit of God to defend our faith. This faith still exists today because of men who, through their relationship to God's Word, became mighty men of valor. These men were not only willing to die for their faith; they did die for their faith.

If a preacher is not preaching from his pulpit that all humanity is facing imminent Spiritual danger, then I question where his body, mind and Spirit are. No true man or woman of God is without a sense of urgency in his or her Spirit during such a time as this. Too much of the seed of God's Word has been sown among the thorns from the pulpit. Christ warned that the worries of the world and the deceitfulness of riches have choked off the life in the Word preached, and therefore, rendered those words, regardless of how true they are, fruitless. There are no thirty or sixty or one hundred-fold fruits coming out of most churches today. Call me a fool! Tell me the names of the unsaved people who are new members of your congregation today because of dynamic, convincing, Holy Ghost-inspired preaching, teaching and evangelism.

This is not an assault on your pastor, people; this is a Holy assault on all of Christianity today, preachers and lay people alike! *"Just like a woman who treacherously departs from her lover, so have you departed from Me, declares the Lord!"* (89) God is a jealous God. Does a woman get angry when she discovers her husband has been unfaithful? How much more should the God of Holiness and righteousness, the King of Kings and the Lord of Lords, be angry when He discovers that his beloved (us) have been unfaithful?

This book is a warning of love from God. God did not have to speak to you in this way today, but He does so in order to preserve your life; He has also done so, so that all will clearly be without excuse. The present situation in our world today is at a climax of Spiritual adultery. The nations are all being infiltrated by Spiritual evils. Just hours ago I watched a Christian news report on the millions of Muslim immigrants flooding European countries. In one of the countries, for example, there are now seven Muslims for every Jew. The Muslims are protesting and demanding that the Arabic language be nationalized there. They were visitors but are now are pushing domination.

The religion of Islam is creating worldwide crises. Their beliefs are abhorrent to our Lord and Savior, Jesus Christ. Light and darkness cannot peacefully dwell together. The spirit of Islam hates Israel and, in turn, hates us because America is Israel's number one supporter.

During the 2016 Presidential Campaign, I only heard one man mention the spiritual needs of our Country – Ben Carson. Thanks Ben!

When the situation of the epidemic growth of Islam is viewed from Spiritual eyes, these eyes see nothing but an upcoming cataclysmic catastrophe. As I viewed that news report, shot live in Europe, my Spiritual warning flags went up everywhere. The protests I saw were just the birth pangs of the monster being born.

I can't seem to find any words in the English language to describe the vexation of my Spirit. The only similar situation I can find is that of Isaiah being commanded to preach to a nation that was about to be destroyed. God had already told Isaiah that the preaching would have no consequence. It's a lost, empty, sorrowful feeling, similar to Jeremiah's broken Spirit and sadness as he watched the hand of God moving down from heaven to implement judgement on a sinful and wayward nation.

I see the declining Spiritual welfare of America, in particular, and the boiling pot of Holy wrath facing our nation. The boiling pot is filled with *"fury and indignation and trouble accompanied by "a band of destroying angels."* (90) I hear ringing in my soul over and over again, the words of our Lord, spoken through Asaph, *"Oh that My people would listen to Me, that Israel* (We Christians are Spiritual Israel today, inheritors of that promise) *would walk in My ways and turn My hand against their adversaries."* (91) Truly these words, these cries, of the Holy Spirit are desperately trying to reach the ears of anyone who will listen.

Asaph, in the Spirit with his eyes wide open for God, senses the shrewdness of the enemy that was causing an uproar, much like Islamic fanatics instigating holy war today. He speaks to God and beseeches Him to intervene in a situation which, as I read the words of his plea, may just as well be the words coming out of my mouth, as I speak to our nation:

"O God, do not remain quiet; your enemies make an uproar (Islam) and those who hate You have exalted themselves. (If a person doesn't love Christ, he or she then hates Him.) *They make plans against Your people and they conspire together against your treasured ones.* (If 9/11 wasn't a shrewd conspiracy, then I've never seen one.) *They have said,*

'Come, let us wipe them out as a nation!'" (92) No one can disagree that "Jihad's" ultimate purpose is to wipe us out as a nation." They are convinced that Allah is one hundred percent behind them. Well, Allah may be, but God isn't. Look at North Korea's leader. He's a nutcase with his hand on a trigger, and it's not the trigger of a gun! People were actually putting their hope in the thought that a pro ball player, Dennis Rodman might talk sense to that fool!

It appears to me that Christians and Muslims are both in for a big surprise: Christians, when they realized that they missed the Lord's warning of his soon return and Muslims when they realize The Christ, is God, and the Muslim martyrs find out that there are no virgins as a reward for where they are going!

God is about to shake the foundations of misconceptions throughout the world for both Christians and all those who have followed false prophets to their demise. God is about to make clear that He alone is the Lord and the *"Most High over all the earth!"* (93)

Christianity has had almost 2000 years to conform to the image of God's Son. How have we done in this respect as God's people? When was the last time you met someone who emulated the characteristics of Christ by both word and deed? This is something that all of us need to strive for every day in our Christian lives. It's done by the power of the Holy Spirit through a life whose food is the Word of God. It's that simple! The Holy Word of God is the life-blood of all creation. In it, we live and move and have our being!

The Word of God is everything. It is our "all" as a nation and for the world. The one passage of Scripture which, I feel, is the least understood in all of Christianity is John 1:1, "In the beginning was the Word and the Word was with God and the Word was God." (94) If only people would receive the true revelation of the words, "and the Word was God." Anyone who fully understands these words realizes the indescribable gift we have in the written Word of God. The Word of God is Christ incarnate. Only by faith does one understand this concept. It helps to realize that not only are Christ and His Word one and the same, but they are both living and active now.

The Holy Bible, the Word of God, is as alive as the person reading these words. One must believe in the Christ to recognize this great truth. When an individual feels as though the Word of God is speaking to his heart let me be clear, it was Christ Himself who has spoken. You cannot separate Christ and the Word of God. This is what cults do.

The moment one removes Christ from the Word is the very moment when it is no longer *living and active*. That which was once referred to as the mystery of God is no longer a mystery. The resurrection of Christ and the Written Word have unveiled the mystery for all eternity of the one and only True God's plan for the salvation of all mankind. *"No one comes to the Father but by Me!"* (95) When "the word was God" becomes a living reality in a Christian's life; the Word of God undoubtedly becomes his most valuable treasure.

If the Word is not your most valuable treasure, then you need to pray for revelation and speak with those who know God intimately. These individuals have Christ living within themselves, and there is no disguising it.

It was the Word of God, which transformed my life. I was institutionalized on and off for a period totaling thirty years. During these years, approximately eight of which I spent behind bars, became for me the dearest, most peaceful and treasured years of my life. I was alone with God, I and His living Word. I am living proof of the Spiritual resurrection. The Heavenly Father infused into my very soul the life and breath of His only Son, the Christ.

No one can ever take away from me this gift of undeserved favor. I also *"found His Words and I ate them!"* (96) I've come to a point where I cannot function without my Lord's Word. Without the Word, I feel lifeless, the same way many in our dying world feel today. I, too, was dead, but now I live with Christ as my drive and the motivating factor behind all I do and say.

He is my all in all, my everything. After thirty years, I finally understand the parables of the hidden treasure and the pearl of great price. I must quickly share these with the reader. I'm overwhelmed with joy, knowing that I have finally found the True Treasure. *"The Kingdom of heaven is like a treasure hidden in the field, which a man found and hid; and from joy over it, he goes and sells all that he has, and buys that field."* (97) And also, *"Again the Kingdom of heaven is like a merchant seeking fine pearls, and upon finding one pearl of great value, he went and sold all he had, and bought it!"* (98)

When an individual gets a real and undistorted view of the power of Christ and His forgiveness, there is nothing comparable in value to be found on this earth. *"To live is Christ!"* (99) There simply is no other way, *"And there is salvation in no one else; for there is no other name under heaven that has been given among men, by which we must be saved."* (100) This obviously makes the names, *Allah* and *Muhammad,* null and void in regard to eternal life.

The importance of God's Word can never, ever, be overstated. This is an impossibility! It's the lack of the knowledge of God's Word amongst his people, which sorrows our Father's heart. He knows that without this knowledge lurk the vessels of death. His prophet warns us even today when he says, *"My people are destroyed for lack of knowledge."* (101)

The one and only hope for America and the world is the Word of God, Jesus Christ, *"the Way the Truth and the Life!"* (102) Without Jesus, the truth is a lie; the way is wrong and life equals death, period. Without Light, the world remains in darkness, no matter how bright the sun seems to be shining in your neighborhood. If you can't see Christ, you're blind. If you can't hear Christ, you're deaf. If you can't find Christ, you're lost. If you can't read God's Word, have someone read it to you.

Approximately twenty years ago, while I lay in a jail cell with about four months left on my sentence, the Holy Spirit began to speak to me in a strange way. It was approximately two A.M. and I heard a voice speaking a message, which captured my attention. This continued for at least fifteen minutes. The message was only growing more serious as each minute went by. I suddenly felt a prompting to get out of bed and write these words down as the voice spoke them. I, however, was totally exhausted and certainly was not thrilled about getting out of bed to take dictation. Besides that, this utterance had already gone on for fifteen minutes or so. My thought was "God, you know I'm exhausted and the only way I'm getting out of this bed and writing is if You bring this exact message back word for word from the beginning so that I know it's Your will. Otherwise, I'll just consider it just an act of my own mind doing Spiritual contemplation of some kind. I'm just so tired.

Now remember, reader, I had just interrupted what was a fifteen-minute dialogue, which was as clear as a tape recorder. The only problem was there were no rewind buttons to push. I simply had an easy enough solution. Only God could bring this back to me verbatim from the beginning.

I lay my head back down after sitting up from my frustration. Low and behold, within one minute it started again. I leaped out of bed and sat at my little steel workbench/desk and began to write.

I never stopped moving my ink pen once until I had over half of this manuscript handwritten in front of me. My index finger literally had a dent in it, which stayed for at least three hours after I had put the pen down. I wrote as fast as I could and never missed a single word. My handwriting was quite sloppy, but I knew I could read my own Egyptian hieroglyphics later. When I had finished, I knew I had just been given a very serious message from God. Now the big problem, what was I supposed to do with this seemingly prophetic message? Well, I did what the Spirit directed me to do. Nothing, at least, not yet!

I felt like I was holding a hot potato. I figured that if God could speak to me while I wrote for hours upon hours, He would also speak to me and tell me what to do with this message and when. Believe me, I was watching daily for God's directives and chomping at the bit to preach this message or publish it, but I also knew the vitalness of following God's prompting in order for the message to be effective. I waited and waited. Two years passed and I hadn't heard a peep.

I should also inform the reader of what had taken place in the four months prior to my recording the message. I had just finished handing out over 400 Bibles in the institution, and through this gift of evangelism, I was able to watch the Bible study group in the facility go from three inmates to close to fifty-four. I spent every waking hour during that one-year sentence studying Scripture, praying, bringing men to Christ, teaching Scripture and visiting the chaplain's office. The Holy Ghost gave me a tireless Spirit. I never watched TV and I played only two or three games of table hockey during that time during the entire one-year sentence.

My focus was souls and souls I got. Praise the Lord! My nickname was preacher man, and every soul there, good and bad, knew exactly who I was and where my cell was. I could honestly not count the number of people who came to my cell door to seek counsel or who simply wanted questions about God answered. I even got the occasional wise guy who would holler up from the bottom tier, "Hey, preacher man, this is 208. (A cell number in the joint is like an address.) Is God able to make a rock so big that He can't lift it himself?" I had to take the bad with the good.

My answers to questions like these were usually simple. "God can do anything!" For the most part, the majority of inmates showed me a tremendous amount of respect. It was made quite clear to all there, including the staff, that I wasn't *playing church.* I was a force to be reckoned with, especially when confronted by learned Muslims or any other non-Christian religious group.

I had the sword of the Spirit strapped on at all times, ready for war. I never lost one battle. How could I? *"Greater is He that is in me that he that is in the world!"* (103) God gave me a fearless faith, I mean *fearless!* I know it was God because I didn't weigh a speck over 140 pounds. One of the biggest, bulkiest, strongest inmates in the facility, who had basically no contenders, a former Muslim, (Notice that I said "former") and a very high-ranking gang member was watching me very closely every day.

I knew well he was doing this because I was always on the alert. He approached me first with small talk. He was African-American. I was white. The only reason I even mention this is because, under the circumstances, the two of us together was very unusual, especially because he was a gang member and I wasn't. Red flags went up all over and both of us heard the comments from all sides. It was clear to me that Mike wanted what I had far more than he wanted to please his gang associates.

He had two things going for him though: one, he was the highest-ranking member of his gang in the facility and he was, by far, the toughest. I was the only white, non-gang member ever to sit at all of the following tables during chow: Vice Lords, Gangster Disciples or GD, Native American and Bloods! This alone was a miracle of New Testament proportions. I sat down right next to Mike at one of the above gang tables and just watched everyone in the place waiting for the fight to start. Little did any of them know that God had already won the fight for me in the battle for Mike's soul. Many of the gang members at Mike's table clearly were not happy with me sitting there amongst them. Many of them told me to my face, "You need to move!" Mike straightened that out with a simple, "He's with me!" It was very uncomfortable at first, but after becoming one of them on a regular basis, things remained "fairly" cool! Not perfectly, just "fairly" cool.

During the next few months, Mike and I became inseparable. Not only did he publicly renounce Allah and Mohammed and the Koran, he began literally forcing the young gang members to attend church with him in the chapel Sunday mornings! He did this "forcing" by order of his gang rank and not physically. He retained his gang status just long enough to use it fully for God's Kingdom!

The first Sunday he must have had nine or ten young gang members with him in the Chapel, sitting in the back. I was so filled with joy when I looked behind myself, I could only say, "Praise the Lord" over and over again! Michael also helped me in filling that Bible Study. We had a spiritual blast! The walls of Spiritual Jericho were coming down with a thunderous crash in that jail!

Even the chaplain was blown away. He later called me to his office the day before I was to be discharged and said, "Well, Alan, I don't know what to say! You've sure made my job easy. I just don't know what we're going to do without you!" I was clearly blessed and never expected to hear such words. I give God all the glory for the power in His Holy Word! Jesus saves, not US! I was just an empty vessel who allowed God to fill me with His Spirit and mission. It is truly one of the greatest memories of my life!

I know that God had done a mighty work in Michael's life, especially when about one month after I began sharing Christ with him, he walked down the tier to my cell during a period when all the doors are opened and an inmate can visit with other inmates (about

200 in my block), and he said, "Alan, come down here to my room (cell); I want to show you something." I was comfortable reading at the time and really did not want to go to his room and besides he still had not taken down the fifty or so naked lady' pictures glued to the walls with toothpaste. So, I just said, "What is it? Just tell me."

He said, "Just come on, please."

So, I went. He had a huge smile on his face the whole time and he definitely was not beyond pulling a practical joke, some of which I liked and some of which I did not. To say the least, I was on high alert! Right before we got to his door, he told me to "Shut my eyes!" Now that definitely made me *hinkey*! (A word used to describe a drug dealer when he's beginning to realize that the person trying to buy drugs from him may be a cop) Anyway, now I'm starting to get really concerned because surprises in jail are not like the surprises you might expect on the outside.

So, here I am, blind! Mike's got me by the hand and he leads me into a cell while I wasn't paying attention to the addresses above the doors. Now he says, "Open your eyes!"

Bang, I open them, expecting something spectacular like a pile of fifty Bibles or something but there's nothing. I look around and first realize I'm not in Mike's cell. Getting caught in someone else's cell could be bad, very bad! I nervously say in a dumbfounded way, "What? What's going on? What is it?" By now I want to get out of there before the trouble starts.

Mike is just smiling and he says, "Look around."

I say, "At what?"

"The walls," Mike says, "my walls."

At first, it didn't hit me but it really was Mike's room. All the naked lady pictures and centerfolds were gone, every single one! He even cleaned the toothpaste off the walls. Actually, his room resembled mine. It looked like a mini-chapel.

All I could do was smile and say what I always did, "Praise God," and then I gave him a big hug. It was from that point on that I knew big Mike was a warrior for the Lord. Two weeks prior I had told Mike that he should take his pictures down, but he hadn't been quite ready. He proved his godly warrior skills in the upcoming months.

The best part of this whole story, though, is what happened about four years later. My phone rang one night. On the line was one of the seventy-plus-year-old Bible-study leaders who came in weekly to teach about Christ. He identified himself. I immediately knew who he was. He made some small talk and asked how I was doing. I was honest and began to tell him, as I recall, about some doubts I was going through in regard to my ministry and if I was still needed by God and whether I had lost my gift. I talked about all sorts of demonic attacks.

In retrospect, I was just under what I'm used to now, a Spiritual attack on my faith by Satan, the loser. Anyway, after I expressed my despondency, he said, "Hey, I've got someone on the other line that wants to say hi to you. Hang on."

I had never met any of his family so I was clueless on this one. Next, I heard the word, "Alan!' I knew exactly who this was instantly.

"Mike! Mike! What in the world are you doing?" My despondency turned into joy so fast that it might never have existed for the week or so that I wrestled with Satan. "What's going on, Mike?"

He said, "Well, I felt the Lord wanted me to call you and tell you a few things so that's what I'm doing. Well, first of all, I just graduated from college, (miracle number one) second, I'm married to a Christian woman, (miracle number two) third, I've got a new baby, (miracle number three) and I'm opening up a new business (miracle number four).

Wow! Talk about God sending a messenger angel of encouragement right when my load seemed too heavy to bear. All I could say again was "Praise God, man! This is truly the God I serve!"

Guess what else? About four years later, on a dreary *dark night of the soul*, I was being attacked by the same demonic spirit with the same M.O. Then my phone rings again. This time it's my dad! He begins to explain that he just got off the phone with a girl named Jennifer. My dad's name is Al too. I used to correspond with a girl at the Minnesota Prison for Women. I had shared the Lord with her. For around one year, she had been trying to locate me. She had lost my telephone number and ended getting the number from directory assistance for Al Overline. She called the number. When my dad answered, she assumed she was talking to me and began giving a powerful testimony of what the Lord had done in her life.

Briefly into the conversation, it dawned on my dad that this woman was probably looking for his son. He interrupted her and said, "I think you may just want to talk to my son Alan."

She realized what had happened and laughed. She got my phone number and called me with the following report, "Al, I've been looking all over to find out how to get in contact with you and tell you what the Lord has done. I married a Christian minister and we've had two kids together and we're now in charge of a children's ministry!"

She was such a powerful and encouraging testimony, being a former hardcore heroin addict. Surely the Lord was faithful in completing the work He began in her life. I praise God for another name written in the Lamb's Book of Life!

While I'm on the subject of testimonies, I feel I have to interject the story of a Russian cab driver I met a few months after my release. I was living in an acquaintance's house, remodeling the interior. Because I had lost my driving privileges for a prior DWI (fifteen of them), I always had to hire cab drivers, even for long distance trips. Yes, God heals alcoholics!

On this occasion, I called the cab company and had them dispatch a cabbie to where I was staying. It was to be a long trip, over sixty miles, and I told dispatch that in advance.

A little while later a man named Oleg, a recent immigrant from Russia, who also had brought his wife and children to America, pulled up in the driveway and honked the horn. I got in the car with Oleg and told him my destination and off we went. I began asking Oleg questions about Russia and how he was getting along in the United States and where his wife and children were.

He seemed very polite and eager to talk. Now anyone who knows the history of Russia knows that atheism was the norm for a long period of Russian history. I figured my odds were best that Oleg needed Christ. The best part of all was that I had a captive audience for at least the next two hours, an hour each way. We must always remember, people, 'today is the day of salvation.'

Now before I continue the narrative on Oleg's story, I want to point out how often the Lord makes an opportunity for all Christians to share the glory of His Son. If we, as Christians, are truly seeking daily to share Christ, God will bring the souls to us always. Doesn't the Word encourage us in our mission in the Gospel of John where Christ states, *"And I, if I be lifted up from the earth* (His story told), *I will draw all men unto Myself!"* (104) All we have to do is be willing and full of the Word. God will do the rest.

As Oleg and I were driving down the interstate, I began to question him in regards to his religious beliefs. It was quite clear from his responses that he really had none. I didn't attempt to lead him from Genesis to Revelation but rather excitedly shared with him the facts about eternal life.

I said, "Oleg, I've got a question for you. If you got in a bad car accident after you dropped me off, do you know where you're going?"

Oleg answered, "Not really."

I asked, "Well, isn't that kind of a scary way to live? If I die tomorrow, I know exactly where I'm going and for how long. This I'm one hundred percent positive about, Oleg."

Oleg responded, "Well, how do you know that?"

Little did he know that he had asked my favorite question.

It opens the doors wide for the good news of Christ's sacrificial death and the benefits of His resurrection!

Oleg listened quite intensely, so much that he was having a difficult time focusing on his driving. He was far more interested in my words than whether we might crash. (Maybe he figured he was already saved from the excitement of just hearing about Christ.) Anyway, after thoroughly explaining God's plan of salvation, I also explained to him how one simply asks Christ to come into their hearts and He begins to clean up the mess we have created over years of living in sin without Christ. I also made it clear that without Christ hell is as real as the 'meter reading' Oleg would check when I left his cab. I explained Hell in such a way that he surely wanted no part of it. After I gave him all this information, he probably had plenty to think about. I didn't feel led to go immediately into *The*

Sinner's Prayer. Rather I just told him that after he dropped me off, when he'd be alone with God in his car, that all he had to do was ask Christ to come into his heart, and if he was sincere, God would know and would, in fact, do just as Oleg had asked.

I made this comment about eight or so miles from my house. Feeling quite confident that the Lord had honored my request for a new name written down in glory, I took the last few minutes to share with him the importance of sharing this with his wife and kids because, "After all, Oleg, you certainly wouldn't want to go to heaven and leave them behind, would you?"

Oleg agreed, "Yes that's a good idea!"

So now I arrived home. I got out of the car and said, "God bless you, Oleg. I hope to see you and your family in heaven someday. Goodbye!"

I shut the door and walked through the overhead garage door and toward the service door leading into the house. I said, "Lord, I hope he prays this prayer!"

Just as I was about to grab the knob and turn it, something happened which had never happened to me before, nor since. It was identical to the words of Peter as recorded in Luke 11:5. *I was in the city of Joppa praying, AND IN A TRANCE I SAW A VISION!"* (105) As I grabbed the doorknob, my body stopped and I was immediately in a trance-like state and I saw a vision!

I saw myself in this vision. I was in heaven standing in a long line, which seemed as if it had no end, as if I were looking at the ocean. I was fairly close to the judgement throne where I saw the Lord on His throne with a brightness around it.

I couldn't hear any words, but the atmosphere was electrifying. I had a very calm, but expectant, Spirit, as I waited to meet the Lord face to face and hear the words I've waited for my whole life. "Well done, my good and faithful servant. Enter now into the Kingdom of Joy, which I have prepared for you and the Angels!"

While I was waiting in line, I decided again to look at this vast and endless, neat, single-file line of people behind me. As I turned around, I really couldn't see many faces because the line was so long and perfectly straight. All of a sudden, from what seemed to be about twenty-five yards behind me, came Oleg, leaning out to the side, with a radiant smile on his face, waving to me with his right hand in the air.

My heart was overwhelmed! I woke up holding the doorknob in my hand crying tears of unexplainable joy! I hadn't even reached the house and the Lord had worked a miracle for me and answered the question on my heart. "Lord, did I win another soul, another name for the Lamb's Book of Life?"

I have related this experience to the reader exactly as it happened. Give God all the glory, for He alone is worthy to be praised. Amen!

Now, just one more personal story I must share with you that happened while I was in prison when my mother died. This is very personal, but the Lord put it in my heart to share it with you. One day in prison, halfway through a sentence, one of the guards called my name over a loudspeaker and told me to report to the desk area.

He said, Overline, you have a phone call in phone booth #2. Now mind you, we never get incoming calls in prison. I had absolutely no idea what was going on!

I picked up the phone and said "Hello!" I then heard my fathers voice, usually which is very strong, say in a somber voice, "Alan, this is your dad calling (as if I didn't know). We are all here at the nursing home with your mother and the clergy here has just given your mother her last rites." Within seconds of that announcement, I heard my mother take her last breath!

Now I must tell you here, never once did I hear my father cry. Before he did I began saying over and over again, "Dad, I'm so sorry that I can't be there for you. I'm so, so, sorry dad!" Then I began to cry profusely! Within 30 seconds into my crying I heard these exact words come out of my fathers mouth while weeping, "Son, you don't have to be sorry; I'm so proud of you! You have brought more people to Christ, than any man I personally know. Of all my 5 children, you are my shining star! I love you!"

After 8 years behinds bars people, these words empowered me beyond description. My father knew the eternal value of my work for Christ! That was more important to him than all the temporal things we go through in life! Even during the saddest part of his life, after watching my mother die slowly of Alzheimer's disease for probably eighteen years, still at the forefront of his mind was God's will!

I would like, at this point, to bring the reader back to complete my narrative in regard to the prophetic type of message the Lord had given me in jail, the message which I had been holding for two years and had not yet been directed to release. I had just felt it necessary to describe to the reader in some detail the Spiritual atmosphere and blessings I was receiving during that time in jail so as to let the reader know my Spiritual state when I received the message from God. I had been walking with the Lord, as I stated before, almost every waking moment during that period of my life. I guess God saw fit to trust me with what I felt was a very powerful and urgent message, and, to me, that's all that mattered.

As I stated before, I just had to wait for God's timing. It would have been disobedient and arrogant to release this message prematurely. I know now that this message was for God's twenty-first century Christians. I had waited ten years for its unhindered release, and right after the problems in Iraq began, God unequivocally prodded me to release the message. Only once, about 20 years ago, did the Lord allow me to share the message with a small congregation in Florida, prior to its full release now, 2016.

The circumstances surrounding the first release were simply a miracle! Anyone reading this book who had sat in that church that Sunday morning would completely agree. I don't recall the name of the city in which the reading took place because for five years I traveled all over the United States installing department store fixtures. There were too many cities, but I believe it was near South Palm Beach.

Nevertheless, this is what took place: It was an early Sunday morning, I was living with about eight other men who were also fixture installers. When I awoke, everyone else was sound asleep. The individuals I was working with did a lot of drinking, especially on Saturday nights. I was the only one who didn't use alcohol. I had been "dry" for quite an extended period of time prior to my arrival in Florida. Witnessing the drinking was hard on me, but I did my best to walk with God. Around 7:00 A.M. I left the house alone to look for a church service. I had absolutely no idea where anything was. I had memorized the directions to our job site but that was all.

I proceeded to drive down the main thoroughfares to avoid getting lost. I was confident that I would find a church not too far from the beaten path. I was probably about four miles from where we stayed when a very peculiar thing happened. I drove by a building, which resembled a school of some type. There was only one lone car parked out front. The Lord directed me to pull in, so I did.

As I walked in through the school doors, I entered an area where I found a single man going about his duties. I noticed a lot of chairs lined up as if for a church service.

What happened, only God can explain.

I asked the man, "Is this a church?"

He said, "Yes."

I continued, "Is the pastor here?"

"I'm the pastor," he said.

"The Lord has asked me to come and give a message to your people this morning."

(I should let the reader know that up to this point I had never preached a sermon or spoken in church in my life.) For whatever reason, I don't recall even the slightest nervousness or hesitation in my words. I had no intention whatsoever of saying anything. The words just came out.

The man calmly looked at me and said, "I will let you know my response after worship. Please join us."

I said, "OK."

Immediately it occurred to me what I had just said. Message? What message? I don't have a message. What's going on?

I walked outside by my car and it hit me like a brick. A message. The "MESSAGE." My heart started to pound as it were trying to come through my chest. The message from God which I had recorded eight years earlier was at the house in my briefcase. I never left my hometown without this message or my Bible in my possession. Fires happen every day and I wasn't about to lose my treasured Bible nor this message! I had kept it from harm for many years! I jumped in my car and made a beeline back to my temporary residence to get the message.

A few of the guys were awake and were wondering where I'd been and where was I going in such a tizzy.

I said, "To church. You wanna go?"

The answer was a unanimous. "No!"

I bolted. Back to the church I hurried with the message in hand. The message had a title, **This Life! Hour by Hour A Life and Death Crisis**. You are about to read it at the end of this book!

I walked into the church just in time. The service has not yet begun, but all the seats seemed full. I'm sure the pastor must have wondered where I had disappeared, but he never mentioned anything.

As I contemplated the situation, I wondered if this pastor thought he might have encountered a nut case. He had never seen me in his life. Nevertheless, I sat down and worshipped with the congregation for around thirty minutes. The pastor had promised to tell me his response after worship. There I sat wondering how this would all work out.

He began reading the weekly announcements and I listened patiently. I can't really say I was calm at this point because God had put me in a very peculiar situation. However, I did recognize the voice of God and the prompting of the Spirit as clear as a bell. At least, I had always recognized them in the past. Would today be any different? Did I get off in the flesh somewhere and leave my heart at home? Those very questions were about to be answered irrefutably.

After the announcements, the pastor spoke. "Something very unusual has happened this morning. All week long I struggled to write a message for this Sunday. I went around and around with God and kept on coming up empty-handed. I tried repeatedly and still kept drawing blanks. I actually came here this morning as your pastor without a sermon prepared. I just couldn't figure it out, but God himself has provided for us this morning. Before the service started this morning, a man who is seated among you walked in and told me that God had sent him here to give my people a message. I guess that explains why God gave me nothing over and over again this week. I would like to introduce our guest."

WOW! All I can say is WOW!

This was God. I followed His directives, by faith, to the nth degree and, low and behold, I'm now standing on a pulpit in a church in Florida with a group of people I've never seen before, a church I've never been to before, with a message the Lord had given me many years earlier.

I opened my folder with the words, "***This Life***" staring me in the face. The congregation was waiting with bated breath. The Holy Ghost filled me with a fervor I had never known. I preached that message as if it were the only one left on earth and Christ was returning tomorrow.

I preached for two hours and fifteen minutes and barely stopped to breathe. You could have heard a pin drop on the carpet. After I finished, I sat back in my chair. There was a still and silence as if Jesus had calmed a storm.

The pastor was awed and so was everyone else, including me. I had survived. There was a Holy hush in the room. I heard whispers around me at least three times.

"He's a prophet."

"This man's a prophet."

"A prophet!"

I shook ten or twenty hands outside the church and left, blown away by what God had orchestrated. Jesus is the Lord of Divine Providence. I don't know about all this prophet stuff. The only thing I know was that I had been obedient when God performed a miracle.

Only two days later I was giving God the glory for this miracle while at a laundromat about two miles from our rented house. I had met some man there with his kid, and I began sharing this miracle with him.

He was a full-blooded Haitian and a minister from an Assemblies of God church called Full Gospel Assembly. While I was sharing Christ's power with this total stranger I had no idea who or what he was. (People ask if I do this all the time with strangers. The answer is yes, I do, and so should you.)

Anyway, after about twenty minutes into our conversation, this man asked me point blank out of the blue, "How would you like to come and preach in our church on Wednesday night?"

I asked, "What? Are you a pastor or something?"

In his Creole accent, he answered, "Yes, I am."

He gave me directions and a time to be in his church. No one in this world could describe my feelings. I had been praying for years, literally years, for God to release me to preach and the next thing I knew the opportunities are coming out of the woodwork.

That night I did not preach ***"This Life."*** God never directed me to do so. This was my second time on a pulpit in three days, the first two times in my life. This time, however, I spoke from the heart without a script, none whatsoever.

To top the situation off, I looked like a marshmallow sitting on a coal pile. I was the only white guy there amidst approximately 250 Haitians, and I had to preach through an interpreter. God is just hilarious.

The experience was awesome, however. Now I knew why God didn't have me preach the other message. The interpreter would have been tongue-tied. Besides that, the church didn't let out until almost midnight.

Praise the Lord! I had preached for about fifteen minutes. I have yet, to this day, ever seen any group of people worship from their hearts like the Haitian people. I guess poverty does have its privileges, America. From this, we could all learn a valuable lesson in unhindered, grateful worship.

Now for the message I've waited twelve years to share with you.

The End

The conclusion, when all has been heard: fear God and keep His commandments, because this applies to every person.

For God will bring every act to judgment, everything which is hidden, whether it is good or evil.
Ecclesiastes 12: 13-14

About the Author

Alan Overline is first and foremost an Evangelist; second, a reformer and third, an apologist. His first encounter with scripture was at age thirteen at the Redwing State Reformatory for Juveniles, where he was locked up for waywardness. The only thing in his single cell was a steel bunk and a table to write on where there was a Gideon Bible, which he read from Genesis to Revelations. This is where his love for God's word began.

At age fourteen Alan lasted one week in a foster home as he was suspended from his new school the first week for disrupting class. Soon thereafter, Alan was sent to a boy's home and another new school. At this school Alan focused on his schoolwork and received the highest grades ever.

Returning back to his hometown, Alan started 11th grade but quit about halfway through due to the fact that the same people who disliked him and wouldn't associate with him were still there. When, what would have been his senior year, Alan went to the high school and got all the books needed to graduate by doing the work at home. He received his high school diploma a year later than he would have if he stayed in school. In 1980, Alan opened his own construction business and still operates it today.

Early on in Alan's life, around the age of thirteen, he began using drugs and alcohol. By the time Alan was 18 his alcohol use was already at a chronic stage. This disease took total control over his life and priorities. By the time Al was forty-eight, he had managed to get a total of fifteen DWI's, some of which were felony status. As a result of this, Al spent a total of eight years between jail and prison.

During his incarceration, Al went back to the scriptures for comfort and studied an average of twelve hours a day, seven days a week. During this time, he also read and studied the lives of all the worlds most respected theologians from Thomas Aquinas to St. Augustine, Jerome, Luther and so on. He studied history to better understand human behavior such as Alexander Isayevich Solzhenitsyn's 'The Gulag Archipelago'. If you heard the name, he read it. He also studied Greek and Hebrew and read probably every expository on scripture ever written.

Alan has a photographic memory and can at the snap of a finger quote verbatim a hundred scriptures without a problem. He also studied the great apologists like Dr. Walter Martin and used these writings along with scripture to convert multitudes of cult members, Muslims and gang members, just to mention a few. His poem "The Man in the Shell" has been heard by approximately 30 million people in the US and 40 countries combined. This poem is his life story from start to finish (the short version) and how Christ saved him from a sure death. The book you are about to read, *This Life,* is the culmination of all his studies and what God has revealed to him during his time of incarceration and still today. Alan addresses the demise of the morality of America as a once great spiritual nation and how we can restore theocracy. The word of God itself is put on a pedestal and personal devotion to it or more so, the lack thereof, is the number one issue that he sees as why we are so weak and have lost our holy influence individually and as a nation!

Alan's spirit of reformation is clear throughout the entire book as is his love for souls and the need for Evangelism. Also, he addresses the destructive spirit of materialism and playing church for selfish reasons. Dr. Ken Chant, born in Australia, planted eight churches, pastored several others, editor of two Pentecostal journals, principal of four bible colleges – United States and Australia, received a medal in the Order of Australia (OAM), General Division, and in the Queen's Honours list. He authored forty books, President of Vision Christian College (Australia), and is on the International Board of Directors for Vision International University (USA). Dr. Chant has been in ministry for over fifty years. He was also the associate pastor for five years of what was then the largest Pentecostal church in Australia! The Adelaide Crusade Centre.

It is this man who first read my husband's manuscript because Alan held this man in such high esteem. Alan always said Dr. Chant was hands down the best preacher he ever heard and attributed this due to his great love for God's word! He said that he made it his practice to read through the entire Bible once every year! Henceforth, his gift of **DYNAMIC PREACHING!**

My husband was truly honored to have such a fine man of God do the first reading of his book. Not only did he read it, but also when asked by my husband, "Out of all the books you have read in your lifetime, what author would you compare my writing to?" His response stunned by husband! He said, "John Bunyan!" The author of the second most widely read Christian book in the world – *The Pilgrim's Progress*, second only to the Bible. What a surprise and what an honor!

I hope your reading of this book will motivate you spiritually as it has me.

Sincerely,
His wife, Susan

CPSIA information can be obtained
at www.ICGtesting.com
Printed in the USA
FSHW011400300321